Triumph in the Trenches

Triumph in the Trenches

The Green Book for Black Professionals

Edited by Elona Washington
Publisher: The Author's Journey

Contributing Authors

Rev. Dr. Xenia Barnes
Pamela Buchanan, MD
Dr. Mary Darden-Robinson
Leila Lawson
Professor Shakira Releford
Dr. Sherone Smith-Sanchez
Glynnis Swan
Carolyn Wells
Phillip Woolfolk
Dr. Carrie Young-McWilliams

Dedication

To every worker, leader, and changemaker who refuses to be broken by toxicity and systemic oppression: May you find strength in your voice, courage in your convictions, and power in your resilience.

Table of Contents

Foreword

For far too long, we've been told to shrink ourselves, to sacrifice who we are just to fit into spaces that don't even value us. As Black professionals, we've been asked to prioritize the needs of the businesses and companies we work for at the expense of our sanity, livelihood, and personhood. Then, from 9 AM to 5 PM, we're microaggressed and macroaggressed, as if enduring them was in the fine print of the job description when we applied for what we thought was our dream role.

This constant racism has come at a cost—leading to higher levels of anxiety, depression, burnout, social isolation, irritability, hypersensitivity, and hypervigilance. All because we've been trying to survive in a system built to make us feel less than, all while just trying to make a living.

Triumph in the Trenches: The Green Book for Black Professionals serves as one of the solutions to help us make sense of this capitalist calamity we're entrenched in. It provides us with language, strategies, and a train of thought to persevere, despite this unfortunate reality, by exposing us to the experiences of other professionals who have faced similar struggles.

"Did she really just say that to me?"

"Did he mean it that way, or am I tripping?"

Our minds often race as we replay conversations, analyzing all the ways a statement could have been intended or interpreted. After a while, we start to see what W.E.B. DuBois meant by double consciousness—the constant juggling of how we see ourselves versus how the world sees us. That twoness he spoke of slowly merges into a oneness that exists solely to serve the dominant society, causing us to forget who we were before we clocked in.

"Who am I?"

Am I the person I present myself to be during those eight hours, or am I the person who slowly reemerges as I walk out the door—grabbing my phone, venting to a friend about the latest psychological scar and bruise left by them White folks?

At some point, we all hit a breaking point. Like Fannie Lou Hamer said, we grow sick and tired of being sick and tired. The high blood pressure, the headaches, the insomnia—these are signs that the baggage is too heavy to bear. It's begun to wear you down long after those eight hours of hell. Racial battle fatigue has consumed every aspect of your life, to the point where even your spouse and kids feel anxious around you, sensing the weight you carry but not knowing how to help.

"I had a rough day at work today. Just gimme a second."
Enough is enough. Your health is suffering. Your mind is suffering. And now, your family is suffering. Something's gotta give. Either you muster the courage to speak up or leave but staying complacent and complicit is no longer an option.

Right now, while systemic oppression and workplace inequities are out in the open, the very words and terms we've always used to speak on our struggle—or to carve out better paths for ourselves—are getting twisted into dirty words by politicians with agendas. In the midst of all that, this book stands as a beacon of hope. It is a reminder that we are not the problem. The problem is the system and the treatment we've endured.

Triumph in the Trenches: The Green Book for Black Professionals is more than a guide—it's a lifeline, a source of validation, and a call to action for all of us navigating these trenches. Its strength lies in its authenticity. The contributors don't hold back. They tell it like it is, exposing the harsh realities we face while offering tools and strategies to not just survive but thrive in these oppressive systems. You'll find hope in these pages—hope because you're still here. Hope because you stand on the shoulders of those who fought to get you to this point, so that you can take it another step further for those who come after you.

And for those seeking to be allies and co-conspirators, Triumph in the Trenches: The Green Book for Black Professionals will equip you with a tremendous amount of insight that will create a drastic shift in your workplace approaches and practices, whether you enter the workplace as a colleague or in a leadership position. It is a guide to understanding the biases and blind spots shaped by media, community, and educational socialization, with clear strategies on how to counter them and create a more equitable workplace.

If our country and the world are truly committed to becoming more inclusive and reflective of the diversity that defines our society, then our workplaces—where we spend the majority of our lives—must take active steps to ensure that the unfair practices and realities outlined in Triumph in the Trenches: The Green Book for Black Professionals become obsolete. As such, it should be required reading for all.

So, let this book inspire you, guide you, and equip you for the challenges we endure in this present moment and the road ahead. Together, we can create a world where equity and inclusion are not just aspirations but realities. This is our moment, and this book is our guide. Let's seize it.

Ernest Crim III, M.A.
Emmy-Nominated Producer, Public Teacher, & Author

1

Journey Home

Carolyn D. Wells

In preparing to write this chapter, I created a timeline of my life—from youth to now, 50-plus years. I recalled the cultural experiences, environments, spoken words, achievements, failures, and the people who have influenced my values, self-awareness, and the lens through which I view humanity, which is a healthy view that good-hearted people come in all shapes, colors, and sizes and that we all have the capacity for empathy, kindness, and consideration for others.

I paused to consider that just as my lived experiences have led me to esteem the janitor and CEO with the same courtesy and regard; others may hold an entirely different perception of humanity, also shaped by their upbringing and lived experiences. Good or bad, right, or wrong, as we cement and normalize our beliefs and values, we wear them like a cozy cloak—they become a part of who we are.

Having grown up in diverse surroundings, I cannot imagine what it is like to have to alter my beliefs about any people group—I have danced with them all and have learned to judge others by their character, not by their skin. I have my mom to thank for that early exposure to diverse cultures long before I entered high school.

Today, when I encounter adults who, without any provocation, behave in ways that suggest their upbringing was not as diverse as mine, sometimes I want to give them a big hug, and other times, I disengage, understanding it took many years to knit the cozy cloak they proudly wear, and my brief interaction with them is not sufficient to loosen one thread. My propensity to disengage from such individuals has increased as I have aged—another thread that runs through our tightly knitted cloaks.

In my earlier years, I was diligent in calling out injustices and workplace discord. I wanted everyone to get along, and I cared enough to invest the time and patience to break down the walls that kept us siloed and disconnected. What follows is a condensed version of such an encounter, the lessons that I learned from the experience, and my current disposition.

ALLYSHIP

I was the only Black woman in our Midwest office, and to say my onlyness created loneliness would be a severe understatement. The concept of inclusivity to most in this environment meant saving the meeting leftovers for the uninvited.

Microaggressions hurled freely from the mouths of those appointed as leaders. Their attitudes and behaviors trickled down the ranks. "What decade is this?" I wondered. I did not want to end my employment. I enjoyed the work I did and the impact it made on others' lives.

The convenience of a short commute temporarily sweetened the sour reality that I did not belong here—not because of some shortcomings of mine but because I deserved better. I deserved to work in a fair and psychologically safe environment. I deserved to be included and to be authentically ME without feeling as though being myself was not good enough.

Not wanting to start a job search in the wintertime, I decided to embody my mother's peaceful yet purposeful essence and sought ways to spark conversations with those who I would typically only engage transactionally—to complete a project. "How could I influence change in this male-dominated environment?" I thought. I was not prepared to take on the entire organization. My sole goal was to spark a shift in my department—to hopefully bring down the walls that kept us self-interested and disconnected. Thankfully, I had an ally in a senior leader. I requested a meeting and asked if I could share some observations and solutions that could improve work relations and performance.

After listening intently, they encouraged me to increase my social engagement with my colleagues. They also encouraged me to host lunch-and-learns focused on improving workplace relations and communication. I had my ally's full support, and over two years, I earned the trust of my colleagues, and we began to see each other differently. In time, and with the guidance of a consultant, we began to relax our guards and engaged in sensitive conversations about our differences and biases.

We started to magnify our shared goals above individual goals. There was a clear change in communication and collective performance within our department. We trusted each other and welcomed and respected everyone's ideas. Other departments began to take notice and followed suit.

This workplace experience taught me the value of allyship and the importance of understanding the role of lived experiences in shaping racial beliefs. Understanding the impact of lived experiences is essential for fostering empathy, promoting cross-cultural understanding, and dismantling racial prejudices. I also came away understanding the influence of my voice to spark change. Though the challenges in our workplaces seem impenetrable and often intimidating, we must not cower down if, indeed, we choose to remain in those environments.

In our endeavors to impact workplace change, is it possible that we are trying to eat the whole elephant at once instead of taking a bite-size approach? If we struggle with changing our own minds and behaviors, should we expect others to embrace new ways of thinking simply because we share data that implies they should? We believe what we believe for distinct reasons, and long-held beliefs are not easily uprooted.

How do we begin to dismantle the strong towers that keep us divided inside and outside of the workplace, and is it our task to own? I have worked in environments where the predominant inherent beliefs were deeply rooted in patriarchal ideals, sameness, bias, and division. These environments are health hazards, psychologically unsafe, and morale killers.

I commend the passion, commitment, and courage of leaders like Vernā Myers, Ginny Clarke, our congressional leaders, and others who are fearlessly leading the charge in impacting workplaces, institutions, and policies through executive leadership training, legislation, DEI training, and other modes of private and public education. Let's continue supporting their efforts.

OPTIONS ABOUND

As I celebrate the magnificent efforts of these brave leaders, I find my fire to continue engaging and dueling on the corporate playground has dimmed significantly. My view of today's corporate playground is much like the playgrounds of our youth. There are sunny days filled with fun, laughter, creativity, and exploration, and less enjoyable days when bullies rise and make their own self-serving rules for play that disadvantage others.

Many thrive in these spaces while others stay and play along until they burn out or choose other career options such as entrepreneurship. While my prevailing attitude about the corporate playground is not directed related to my current work environment, the years of collective damage have taken its toll. Sadly, many of my colleagues and associates are navigating much of the same with feelings of wanting to disengage from corporate America entirely.

My corporate journey has taken more from me than it has added value to my well-being, and as I prepare for my next endeavor, my heart leaps with joy at the thought of doing work that fuels my soul and impacts family structures in a meaningful way—work that aligns with my core values and altruistic aspirations.

I enter this next phase with my eyes wide open. I realize entrepreneurship can present its own set of challenges, yet the path offers specific opportunities and freedoms that are absent in the corporate landscape. For example, having autonomy, the ability to shape one's workplace culture, innovation latitude, psychological safety, and an unlimited income potential that surpasses what is possible in a traditional job.

Too often we allow a false sense of job security to keep us from bringing our deepest and most authentic visions to life. I often wonder, what stories will my children tell their children about me? How did I impact the lives of people in my community and family? These questions and the sobering knowing that life is fragile, and fleeting spark my get-up, and remind me of why I am here. I feel the force within me rising more now than ever before.

It is essential to acknowledge that while entrepreneurism lessens the reliance on diversity, equity, and inclusion (DEI) programs for wealth-building and community economic development, it does not guarantee a psychologically safe space. The same inequities, biases, and toxic behaviors often found in corporate America can follow us into entrepreneurial settings if we are not diligent to address these little foxes early. These dynamics transcend race, color, creed, and religion and can appear even when we set out with the best intentions to build something different.

I do not have all the answers, but I am convinced we can accomplish more for ourselves and communities through our collective efforts. Historically, we have opened doors and achieved far more without reliance on DEI programs and initiatives. Our rich history bears that proof, as do our ongoing remarkable feats from the boardroom to the courtroom.

As we settle into 2025 under a new administration, talks of reversing our civil liberties with an outright disregard for specific people groups beckons us to find solutions outside of fragile traditional institutions and systems. The solution to much of what ails us is in the journey home.

The late great Jim Rohn said, "If you do not like where you are, move. You are not a tree." This quote calls to mind the sobriety needed to make decisions that impact our very existence and livelihood. It is our time to move and journey home.

THE JOURNEY HOME

The journey home is not necessarily a physical destination. It is a mindset, a return to our full acceptance of the truth about ourselves—our rich origin, abilities, and capacity for greatness and self-reliance. To be clear, the message here is not one of division or segregation. It is one of self-preservation, self-determination, and self-empowerment, which we cannot and should not rely on others to provide. We are witnessing what can happen when we entrust our futures to others.

Our thriving and cultural sustainability are directly connected to our desire and commitment to leverage our influences, collective resources, and innovative prowess. Words are powerful, and the words we speak must be life-giving, forward-thinking, and illuminate the good we want to see in each other and our culture.

Let us not buy into the divisive narratives that suggest we cannot work together or that we will not support one another's success. We must not perpetuate the long-held belief that we must be ten times better just to be good enough. That is not true, and we should eliminate such talks from discussions as others could use them to our disadvantage. We are enough, and we can most certainly join efforts for our greater good. Here are three of numerous examples of our successful collaborations:

In the early 20th century, Madam C.J. Walker, a trailblazing Black entrepreneur, partnered with Marjorie Joyner, a visionary white businesswoman, to expand Walker's hair care product line and beauty schools nationwide, providing economic opportunities for countless Black women. Their collaboration bridged divides and demonstrated that a shared vision and mutual respect could create pathways to success that transcend barriers ("National Inventor's Day: Marjorie S. Joyner | National Archives Museum," n.d.).

Art remains a powerful medium for collaboration and solidarity. In Seattle's International District, a bold mural by Vietnamese artist Tân Nguyễn and Black artist Moses Sun declared,

8

"Chopsticks in a Bundle Are Unbreakable," symbolizing Black and Asian unity. Inspired by this message, Leong launched #AZNxBLM, using her TED funds to support artists exploring Black and Asian solidarity. With backing from The Slants Foundation, artist honorariums doubled, amplifying the project's impact, and highlighting the unifying power of collaboration through art (Campbell 2021).

In media and marketing, Black media collectives like Bomesi, B Code, Blavity360, and Group Black have addressed infrastructure and scale challenges by prioritizing collaboration and tech support (Stenberg and Stenberg 2023). By working together, they have expanded opportunities, simplified agency investments, and created sustainable growth for Black-owned publishers.

These examples remind us that collaboration is not just a strategy; it reflects our values and our history. Let us continue to build on this foundation, honoring the legacy of those who came before us and forge new pathways for those who will follow.

Can we make a cultural commitment to pool our precious resources to create inclusive global networks aligned with our community values, rich heritage, and vivid visions? We can, and the time is right now. We can no longer rely on legislation, empty promises, and initiatives that change like the wind for our empowerment.

Why would we continue to circle cycles of the same, hoping for different outcomes? Isn't that the definition of insanity? We live in America, so we cannot disengage from the fight before us—

maintaining our civil liberties and rights. But as we join with our congressional men and women and others in this significant effort, we must simultaneously journey home to fortify our futures with impenetrable pillars that changing legislation cannot topple.

Journeying home demands entrepreneurial fortitude and focus without risk aversion. Haven't we played small and safe for far too long? The gains of journeying home outweigh our current yields. Though entrepreneurially inspired, a collective approach that considers the whole and not just one will take us far. A beloved African proverb—If you want to go fast, go alone. If you want to go far, go together. We cannot go-it-alone; that is the old way. The journey home is inclusive—everyone is necessary.

As we embark on this transformative ascent, adopting a growth mindset will help us see challenges as growth opportunities and not as reasons to retreat. Emotional resilience, adaptability, accountability, and a focus on wellness and self-care are critical at the start and throughout.

Journeying home. Have we seen such a noble endeavor? What sources can we cite to rest these ideals upon to prove their efficacy? Might I suggest the book you are holding, for starters?

To reclaim our future and embark on the journey home, we must take intentional actions that align with our values, foster collaboration, and empower both ourselves and our communities. The path forward is built on practical steps that encourage growth, resilience, and collective progress.

Here are ten key takeaways from this chapter to help guide your journey and inspire meaningful change in your life and beyond.

1. **Embrace Diversity in Your Own Journey**

   Action: Seek out and engage with people from diverse backgrounds and cultures to broaden your perspective.

   Why It Matters: Exposure to diverse experiences fosters empathy, reduces biases, and helps build a more inclusive worldview.

2. **Recognize the Role of Lived Experiences in Shaping Beliefs**

   Action: Reflect on how your upbringing and experiences influence your perceptions and behaviors. Use this awareness to challenge stereotypes and assumptions about others.

   Why It Matters: Understanding yourself helps foster mutual respect and create space for authentic connections.

3. **Allyship Starts with Small, Intentional Actions**

   Action: Build trust and relationships in your workplace or community by initiating conversations and creating opportunities for collaboration.

   Why It Matters: Lasting change begins with fostering trust and breaking down silos in small, focused ways.

4. **Acknowledge the Realities of Entrepreneurship**

   Action: Understand that while entrepreneurship offers freedom, it does not eliminate challenges like bias or inequities. Be intentional about building inclusive and supportive spaces within your ventures.

Why It Matters: Being realistic about the challenges helps you prepare and create a healthier entrepreneurial environment.

5. **Harness the Power of Collaboration**

   Action: Look for opportunities to collaborate with others across industries and communities to achieve common goals.

   Why It Matters: Collaboration amplifies impact and proves the power of shared resources and vision.

6. **Commit to Self-Reliance and Empowerment**

   Action: Invest in your skills, leverage your resources, and build networks aligned with your values and vision.

   Why It Matters: Relying on external systems for empowerment often leads to disappointment. Self-determination creates lasting independence and strength.

7. **Adopt a Growth Mindset**

   Action: View challenges as opportunities for growth, and practice emotional resilience, adaptability, and accountability.

   Why It Matters: A growth mindset helps you navigate setbacks and keeps you focused on long-term goals.

8. **Prioritize Wellness and Self-Care**

   Action: Make time for mental and emotional well-being to sustain your energy and focus.

   Why It Matters: Change and progress require endurance, which is only possible with a healthy foundation.

9. **Use Words That Uplift and Empower**

   Action: Speak and write with intention, using language that inspires confidence, collaboration, and positive action.

Why It Matters: Words shape mindsets and influence how we see ourselves and others.

10. **Take the First Step Toward the Journey Home**

Action: Begin today by identifying one area in your life where you can build community, embrace collaboration, or take steps toward self-reliance.

Why It Matters: The journey home starts with individual actions that collectively create transformative change.

One thing is certain: when we stop imagining the existence we desire, we settle for what is and what has been. We leave our future in the hands of others. My magnificent imagination tells me that others have imagined the same and more. We have not begun to hear of the joyous ideas that will flourish in 2025 and beyond, inspiring us to unite our collective genius for the betterment of our communities and culture.

Let's journey home!

BIO

C arolyn Wells is a Talent Acquisition professional supporting a leading brand in the manufacturing industry. Nestled in the serene heart of the Midwest, when she is not creating memorable candidate experiences, you'll find her penning poetry and crafting inspiring non-fiction works. Get ready to be charmed by her upcoming poetry collection, *Chestnut Butterflies: Poetic Blooms in the Garden of Life*, releasing in April, celebrating National Poetry Month.

Dive into her world at www.chestnutbutterflies.com and let the magic unfold. Don't miss out—this is Carolyn's third anthology project, following the success of *Start Again: Inspiration from the Sunny Side of Adversity* and *Hug Your Pillars: Stories and Poems Honoring Fathers and Father Figures*, both available on Amazon.

2

A Journey of Integrity and Empowerment

Dr. Carrie Young-McWilliams

My story begins with breaking a cycle—a generational curse, some might say. Teenage pregnancy had plagued the women in my family for generations, and none had ever finished college. But I did. I defied the odds, fought through every obstacle, and stood proudly with my degree, ready to change lives. I thought that meant something. Growing up in Meridian, Mississippi—a state rich with history and echoes of struggle—I learned the power of resilience. My grandmother, a woman of quiet but formidable strength, showed me that resilience wasn't just surviving adversity; it was moving through it with purpose. Her example instilled in me the belief that hard work and determination could open any door.

Yet, when I moved to New England, armed with my degree and unwavering passion, I discovered a harsh truth. My skills, talents, and dreams were overshadowed by a system that saw me as just another overqualified minority. In that world, it wasn't about my knowledge or ability to inspire—it was about having the right political connections, a ticket I didn't hold. Despite breaking my family's cycle, I found myself trapped in another: a system that demanded Black women be exceptional just to be overlooked.

COMMITMENT TO EDUCATION

Education was not merely seen as a route to personal advancement in my family—it was perceived as a communal endeavor that could lift us all from circumstances that seemed beyond our control. This conviction was my North Star, guiding me to become the first in my family to attend college. It wasn't just the personal accolades or the diploma that mattered; it was what my success represented—a beacon of hope and possibility for others trapped in cycles seemingly predetermined by economic and social constraints.

When I arrived in New England, far from the familiar rhythms of Mississippi, I entered an academic world that was both exhilarating and daunting. It was here, in this new environment, that I first confronted the stark realities of systemic bias—a jarring contrast to the meritocratic ideal I had grown up believing in.

The richness of diverse thought collided with unspoken yet pervasive barriers, marginalizing voices like mine in spaces of power and influence. Still, I pressed forward, building a career in education that soon positioned me as a dean of students. Leading not just classrooms but an entire school community inspired me to dream bigger, and I set my sights on becoming a principal. Determined to prepare myself, I enrolled in the Harvard Urban Leaders Institute and later earned my doctorate in educational leadership from the

University of Sarasota, fully equipped to navigate the complexities of urban school leadership.

A COLLISION WITH THE INVISIBLE

With administrative experience and advanced degrees in hand, I felt ready to take the next step. Confident in my qualifications and passion for education, I began applying for assistant principal and principal positions. Interviewing felt natural; I knew my worth and what I had to offer. But as rejection after rejection rolled in, a painful truth emerged. It wasn't my skills or credentials holding me back—it was the system. In this New England school district, where I was one of only five minority administrators, leadership wasn't about merit; it was about politics. I didn't have the connections, the invisible currency that carried others forward. Worse, I wasn't seen as the "right fit." Those words lingered like a wound. It wasn't my education or experience being questioned—it was me, my identity, my background.

The rejections weren't just professional setbacks; they were deeply personal. For years, I had believed that dedication and perseverance would carry me forward. I had poured everything into my students, my community, and my role as an educator. But I was colliding with invisible barriers—obstacles that had nothing to do with my ability to lead and everything to do with race and power. The system wasn't built for people like me to succeed. That harsh truth was laid bare when a leader told me plainly, "You will never lead in this district; you are not the right fit." Those words confirmed what I had come to know: the meritocracy I believed in was a myth, and the barriers I faced were as much about perception as they were about politics.

Today, I use my platform as an educational speaker to share my journey, emphasizing the transformative power of education grounded in ethical stewardship. I work to inspire not only the current generation of educators but also the policymakers who decide the fates of educational frameworks, pushing them to recognize the necessity of maintaining ethics and integrity in every decision-making process. Standing in front of diverse audiences, my goal is to ignite a passion for fairness and integrity in education, implanting the seed that education fueled by empathy and ethics can truly reshape lives and communities.

COURAGE IN NEW ENDEAVORS

The transition to New England was not without its trials. Academic success was met with systemic barriers, highlighting instances where influence often took precedence over achievement. This was difficult to reconcile at first. I realized that my prowess in academia did not always correlate to open doors in professional settings. I became acutely aware of the influence of race and the lack of established networks—factors that played a critical role in opportunities granted or denied.

Navigating these waters required personal perseverance and courage. A deeply rooted belief in my capabilities, honed through years of persistence and self-affirmation, allowed me to assert my presence in spaces where voices like mine had historically been minimized or sidelined.

In these spaces, I was deemed fit to serve but never to lead in the way I knew I was capable—as the servant leader I aspired to be. To even maintain my position, I was told I needed to change myself entirely: dress differently, adjust my hair and eyebrows, soften my 6-foot frame to appear less "intimidating" for my male counterparts, and moderate my tone. This was the feedback I received—not about my qualifications, not about my accomplishments, but about my appearance and presence.

The irony was glaring. My students were thriving, outperforming others in the district. Suspensions and expulsions were at an all-time low, and the tangible outcomes of my work were undeniable. Yet none of that mattered. The barriers holding me back weren't about my performance—they were about the unquantifiable biases rooted in structural racism and political gatekeeping. These forces formed an invisible shield, custom-built to keep me confined in the professional trenches, no matter how hard I worked or how much I achieved. It was never about my ability; it was about a system designed to preserve power for those who looked nothing like me.

As a coach and mentor, I now guide educators across diverse environments in finding their own courage. Through workshops and personal sessions, I help them navigate and challenge the inequities embedded within educational institutions, encouraging them to create and maintain supportive learning spheres where every student is treated with dignity and provided with opportunities to flourish. I emphasize that courage is the ability to rise above the circumstance and take principled action, even when such actions are fraught with complexity and opposition.

HOME: YOU LOOK LIKE ME, BUT YOU ACT LIKE THEM

Completing my education and returning to Mississippi was a pivotal moment in my career. It was not merely a geographic return but a philosophical one. I was coming back with new insights and a burning desire to contribute positively to the place I still called home. Immersing myself in the local educational landscape, I soon found that my expertise and perspective allowed me to identify both familiar and new challenges, particularly when I encountered systemic corruption—a revelation that compelled me to reassess not only my professional commitments but my moral ones. Finally, I was among my people—people who knew the struggle firsthand.

Until I was faced with unethical practices within this school district, my convictions were tested to their limits. The realization that funds meant for student enrichment were being mishandled was a personal affront to everything my family had taught me about integrity. I knew that difficult decisions lay ahead, ones that required more than personal courage—they demanded action that aligned with my ethical principles. In this district, located in the poorest state in the nation, seated in the poorest section of the state, the demographics of the teachers, leaders, and students were 99% Black. So why would leaders take resources away from those who mirrored their younger selves? How could a historically marginalized group of adults push students further to the margins? Oddly, there was little time to waste asking questions when I had to get to work.

Reporting the corruption was fraught with potential consequences, both professionally and personally. Despite the risks, I felt an obligation to expose these malfeasances. It was a decision rooted deeply in an understanding that true leadership often involves making the difficult choices that others shy away from—choices that have the power to instigate meaningful change and accountability within organizations.

Today, I use this unique experience to empower other educators who are faced with ethical dilemmas. I accomplish this through strategic coaching techniques, facilitated workshops, and training. Each mentee is led to acquire the skills necessary to navigate this type of organizational challenge. Then I use the experiences and lessons learned to help them develop the necessary skills to uphold their values in similar circumstances. This ensures that the dismantling of these systems continues throughout the country, with these decisions supporting students, institutions, and communities at large.

The answer is complex yet simplistic at the same time—systemic racism feeds off the mindset it has taken captive regardless of skin color. The only antidote for a learned behavior is to unlearn that behavior. I call it a racism detox—an individual's deliberate act of identifying and extracting assimilated racist behaviors and replacing those behaviors with anti-racist behaviors. The battle starts with self.

THE BATTLE AGAINST CORRUPTION: DETAILED EXPERIENCES

Uncovering the extent of corruption within one of Mississippi's school districts was both enlightening and burdensome as the district was plagued with educators who unknowingly operated with a racist mindset. With each new discovery, I felt a growing responsibility to act. The task of analyzing educational data, intended initially to aid student development, unwittingly became the cornerstone of ethical confrontation. I unearthed patterns of deceit— from unauthorized use of funds earmarked for educational purposes to the manipulation of test scores aimed to paint a rosier picture of student achievement.

Confronted with this disturbing reality, my path was clear yet daunting. Each step towards uncovering the truth was met with resistance, yet it affirmed the importance of ethical advocacy. Reporting these injustices demanded a fortitude I was cultivating every day, fueled by a deep sense of duty not only to our Black students but to the integrity of the educational institution itself.

The emotional toll of this process was compounded by professional isolation in the aftermath; I knew it all too well from New England. Yet, it became a defining moment in my career—a testament to the impact one voice can have in sparking systemic change. Corrupt officials were eventually exposed and removed, but the process taught me invaluable lessons about resilience, community advocacy, and the necessity of unwavering trust in my convictions.

Now, woven into every presentation, discussion, and coaching session I have, these lived experiences serve as poignant examples of how standing firm in one's beliefs can lead to transformative outcomes. The need to work within the system to educate the community and help Black students understand how to advocate to debunk stereotypes, mediocrity, and the historical features of how an institution of racism trickles down to them at the classroom level and creates feelings of isolation, anxiety, and failure.

I challenge students, educators, parents, and community leaders to embrace these hard truths, arming them with the strategies and encouraging them to tap into their moral courage to combat unethical practices in their own environments--it begins with self; they must do the work before demanding it from others. Dismantling these structures will lead to the institution's unraveling, creating a more equitable and fair learning environment for all students.

EMPOWERMENT AND LEADERSHIP: EMPOWERING THROUGH EXAMPLE

Armed with the lessons from my career, I developed the S.E.R.V.E. framework. The pre-work is Self, Exposure, Reflection, View, Equip. Then there is the advocacy portion: Surveillance, Expose, Resilience, Vision, and Empowerment, a framework for combating racism in education. These frameworks are not theoretical; they are a pragmatic approach that I now passionately implement in workshops, training sessions, and personal mentorship arrangements.

The ultimate goal of empowerment is captured elegantly in the success stories of educators and institutions that have adopted this framework, leading to noticeable improvements and elevated morale among students and staff alike. Empowerment through example fosters a sense of shared responsibility and encouragement, encapsulating the profound impact ethical leadership can impart.

Implementing this framework equips educators with the tools needed to lift their students while simultaneously nurturing an environment of accountability and trustworthiness among themselves. These values are essential for dedicating ourselves anew each day to serving as inspiration and support for those we educate.

REFLECTION AND FUTURE VISION

Reflecting on the path I've traveled, the struggles faced solidified my belief in the foundational importance of leading with integrity. This belief informs each speaking engagement and professional relationship, driving my mission to imbue educators with the power of ethical principles in leadership.

Looking to the future, I envision an education system transformed by leaders who are unwavering in their commitment to fairness and equity. As both a mentor and advocate, I aim to continue inspiring and equipping educators to enact meaningful change. Ensuring every student has access to honest, empowering education is the legacy I hope to leave.

Through sharing my experiences, insights, and the frameworks I've developed, I endeavor to encourage others to embrace courage and make positive change in their hearts and institutions. Together, committed to integrity as our guiding light, we can create educational systems where fairness is foundational.

In closing, the work entrenched this final framework I will share, and that is C.A.R.E., my namesake framework. It stands for Courage, Advocacy, Resilience and Ethics, as it takes moral courage, skillful advocacy, diligent resilience and moral ethics to rebirth a new self who has unlearned that which was taught to harm you and your community.

Using my personal journey serves as a call to action for dismantling a racist institution that transcends traditional boundaries; establishing the tagline CARE with Carrie, is a reflection of both personal resolve and a shared vision of enduring change. My deepest desire is for the groundwork laid by our dedication to ethics and leadership to blossom into lasting opportunities, ultimately uplifting the lives of those we are privileged to empower.

BIO

Carrie Young-McWilliams, a passionate advocate for social justice and educational equity from Mississippi, now residing in Maryland, has proudly served as a dedicated member of Delta Sigma Theta Sorority, Inc. for 31 years, upholding its commitment to social action by combating educational disparities and inequalities through her work.. With a background deeply rooted in civil rights activism, Carrie brings extensive experience in educational leadership, having spearheaded transformative initiatives in low-performing high schools and led district-wide reform efforts.

Her diverse career encompasses roles as a dean of students, curriculum author, classroom teacher, and presenter at esteemed national forums like the Aurora Symposium and the National Association of Elementary School Principals. Carrie holds degrees from prestigious institutions such as the University of Central Florida, Sacred Heart University, and the University of Sarasota, where her doctoral research focused on student mobility. As the CEO of Young-McWilliams Education Consulting Services, LLC, and co-founder of EmpowerED Solutions by Young & Horner, LLC, she continues her mission to advance diversity, equity, inclusion, and justice (DEIJ) in education.

Connect with Carrie at youngandhorner.org/empowered and via email at carrieempowers@gmail.com.

3

Breaking Unspoken Rules

Professor Shakira Releford

"Janelle walked a daily tightrope between her true self and the version her coworkers expected, navigating a workplace steeped in white fragility and racial bias. Each step was a careful balance, code-switching to survive the microaggressions that threatened to pull her into isolation."

—Shakira Releford

THE RULES

Janelle Nicholas, a 30-year-old Black woman, was the education director at a well-known nonprofit in East-Central Iowa. She had the resume, the skills, and the drive. Janelle's career was marked by a sense of drowning, feeling trapped by unspoken rules that she could never fully escape.

She immediately noticed the subtle differences in her treatment. Her white coworkers' casual remarks about her hair, such as "It's so cool that you can change your hair so often," rang more of polite disapproval than genuine curiosity. Janelle navigated a daily delicate balance between her authentic self and the version her coworkers anticipated, navigating a workplace steeped in white fragility and racial bias. Each step was a careful balance, code-switching to survive the microaggressions that threatened to pull her into isolation.

Janelle was a people pleaser. Her parents taught her early on that being overly polite, accommodating, and agreeable might be a key to survival in predominantly white spaces. Growing up, Janelle's mother emphasized to her that being a Black woman meant facing double the challenges in life. Janelle's brother was given a similar speech but from the lens of being a Black man in America. Raising kids in the 80s and 90s was similar to the challenges of today. A lot of the same struggles of inferiority, prejudices, and implicit bias from white people were constantly projected toward Black people (and other ethnic groups). The advice from her mother felt more like a blueprint for survival in the workforce and society. These ideologies became the core foundation of Janelle's compulsive need to become a people pleaser.

To fit into the organization's "culture," she agreed to do more, stayed late without complaint, and softened her tone when delivering feedback so she wouldn't appear aggressive. This response to professional trauma has been the narrative for over a decade, and she was ready to explode.

The tipping point came during the Diversity, Equity, and Inclusion (DEI) workshop. The executive director paid an outside consultant to facilitate a one-day workshop about implicit bias, systemic racism, and creating a more inclusive work environment. It looked good in theory, but Janelle wasn't sure it would work.

The session opened with the consultant, a middle-aged Black man, sharing his lived experiences and encouraging employees to "speak up" if they ever felt marginalized. Janelle looked around the room, noticing mainly white faces nodding, some clearly uncomfortable, but most just wanting to get back to work or leave. When it came time for open discussion, Janelle cautiously raised her hand.

THE INTERVENTION

"I think sometimes we need to address the unspoken rules that exist here," Janelle said, her voice carefully measured. "There are preconceived notions about the behavior of certain employees, particularly those of color. It feels like our accomplishments are viewed through a distorted lens, regardless of how well we perform." There was an awkward silence. The consultant nodded slowly, and a white colleague chimed in. "I mean, I've never noticed that, but if that's how you feel, maybe we should talk more about it at a later time."

Anger began to build up fiercely. This white colleague had previously confronted her about her tone, behaving as if she was afraid to be in her presence. Janelle was still thinking about the conversation, and her colleague's comment made her snap. She recognized the constricting feeling in her chest as the unwelcome sensation of being politely dismissed. The familiar tightness she felt was the same one that arose whenever her ideas were dismissed in meetings, only to be repackaged and claimed by another white female executive.

The DEI consultant redirected the conversation; but Janelle could tell that he, too, felt a pang in his chest as her comment hung in the air. Janelle's stiff posture and clenched fists hinted at a simmering storm beneath her calm facade, which he couldn't help but notice. He realized, in that moment, that they were communicating without speaking, a shared understanding felt by many Black professionals. They both knew the bitter taste of being sidelined, the deep frustration of speaking the truth only to have it minimized or brushed aside by white colleagues who found comfort in their ignorance. It was the shared experience of knowing how hard it was to keep breathing life into words that others refused to hear.

The DEI training came and went, and little changed. People returned to their comfortable patterns, checking off the "diversity" box without ever confronting the deeply ingrained biases that shaped the workplace. The organization had a few more minority hires, but Janelle knew that wouldn't fix the issue. What was needed was a shift in the organization's culture, not superficial representation.

One afternoon, after a particularly frustrating team meeting where Janelle had again been talked over and her contributions dismissed, Janelle decided something had to change. She couldn't please everyone. She came to the realization that she could no longer compromise her voice and well-being to conform to a system not designed for her.

Janelle began seeing a therapist who specialized in helping marginalized women navigate workplace dynamics. Through therapy, she addressed years of holding back her authentic Black self and her assertiveness, due to a fear of being labeled "angry" or "difficult" or even being perceived as "not Black enough." It was time to establish boundaries and assert her value.

Saying "no" for the first time felt like an act of rebellion to Janelle. Her supervisor had asked her to take on yet another last-minute project, and she responded, "I can't take this on right now. Can I look into this after we finish our assignment at [xyz] school"? Her supervisor paused, clearly surprised by the pushback, but accepted her answer. That night, Janelle felt a rush of empowerment and overwhelm at the same time. She had taken control of her time and energy without guilt, yet her brain spent a lot of time ruminating about what her supervisor had thought of her. "Did I say all the wrong or right things? Will I get fired? Damn, that felt good!" These were all the thoughts that ran through her head.

However, the real test occurred during a board meeting a few weeks later. As usual, she presented her ideas and project updates with confidence, but once again, a male board member attempted to rephrase her suggestions as his own and dismiss her in front of everybody. This time Janelle didn't sit quietly. She took a deep breath, squared her shoulders, and calmly said, "That's what I just said. Let's focus on how we can implement this idea effectively so we can increase retention with our donors."

Thirty seconds of silence felt like 20 minutes. Janelle could see the surprise on her colleagues' and the board members' faces. This wasn't the Janelle they were used to. She stood her ground. After the meeting, the male board member approached her with a half-hearted apology, but she didn't need his approval anymore. The important thing was that she had spoken up and claimed her space.

THE CHANGE

Over the next few months, Janelle continued to push back against the unspoken rules that had once defined her work experience. She stopped code-switching. She no longer felt obligated to soften her tone or shrink her presence. When confronted with microaggressions, she would address them directly, often in private conversations with colleagues, pointing out behaviors that made her feel devalued or like a token representative. Not everyone responded well, but Janelle no longer needed their validation. She learned in therapy that other people's perceptions were not her reality. Her sense of worth came from God, not people, and she desired to remind herself of that every single day.

The organization's DEI efforts dwindled, with fewer workshops, no policy changes, and no meaningful gestures. The culture remained largely unchanged. Janelle realized that real change wouldn't come from top-down initiatives or corporate buzzwords. It would come from people like her, challenging the system and asserting their right to exist fully, without compromise, and the best part is articulating that with confidence.

By the time she turned 31, Janelle had transitioned into a leadership role at the organization. She mentored other employees, particularly women of color, teaching them the lessons she had learned about boundaries, assertiveness, and self-advocacy. She was done being a people pleaser, rejecting the mold that never truly fit her. Janelle had broken the silence, and in doing so, she had reclaimed her power.

RECOGNIZING COMMUNICATION GAPS

In work environments where communication is essential, it's crucial to identify and address communication breakdowns regarding the challenges faced by minorities navigating society's unspoken rules. Nonverbal communication, implicit messages, and microaggressions often cause these gaps, contributing to an atmosphere where subtle cues reinforce exclusion and inequity.

Unspoken rules are often enforced through nonverbal communication, subtly and powerfully. Minorities often experience discomfort or feel unwelcome in professional spaces through cues that aren't vocalized but felt deeply. For example, when a Black employee like Janelle offers an idea in a meeting, the response may not always be direct; instead, it comes as subtle shifts in body language and unpleasant facial expressions. Colleagues may lean away, avert their eyes, or offer a dismissive nod, showing a lack of genuine engagement or interest. These nonverbal signals send an obvious message: "You do not belong."

According to the book, *Post Traumatic Slave Syndrome*, by Dr. Joy DeGruy, these micro-expressions have roots in historical trauma and systems of oppression that have conditioned non-Black individuals to subconsciously see Black voices as less credible or valuable (DeGruy 2017). Nonverbal cues can influence interpersonal dynamics between two communicators (the sender and the receiver), often conveying messages even more potent than spoken words. The nonverbal dismissal minorities face is a form of silent exclusion that can chip away at self-esteem and reinforce feelings of marginalization.

Implicit messages further complicate workplace interactions. While feedback is an essential component of professional growth, the way it is delivered can often reveal underlying biases. Phrases like, "You're very articulate" may seem like compliments on the surface, but they imply surprise at a minority's ability to speak well, rooted in the assumption that articulate speech is unexpected from certain groups. These implicit messages uphold unspoken rules that set different behavioral standards based on race. Researchers have long recognized that communication is deeply embedded with societal structures, with messages carrying multiple meanings influenced by cultural backgrounds. Dr. DeGruy's work highlights how historical prejudices inform modern interactions, causing minority employees to face a double standard that demands more labor to prove their worth.

Microaggressions are another form of unspoken rule enforcement that impacts minorities in the workplace. It's defined as a subtle, often unintentional, form of prejudice. These minor acts of bias communicate exclusion and can reinforce a power imbalance. Microaggressions can range from comments about a minority employee's hairstyle being "unprofessional" to assumptions about their background or competency. The cumulative effect of these remarks creates an environment where minorities feel constantly under scrutiny and are forced to prove their belonging.

Addressing these communication gaps requires intentional efforts to foster understanding and create an inclusive environment. We need to understand that nonverbal cues, implicit biases, and microaggressions aren't minor problems; they represent major obstacles to feelings of belonging. By understanding the layers of meaning in communication and acknowledging the historical context that informs present-day interactions, workplaces can dismantle the unspoken rules that perpetuate exclusion and inequity.

THE SOLUTION

Survival strategies like people-pleasing and code-switching are common for minorities navigating predominantly white workplaces. These behaviors are deeply ingrained and often start early, shaped by the knowledge that fitting in, or, at the very least, not standing out is key to surviving in spaces not designed for inclusion. People-pleasing behaviors in professional settings include taking on unnecessary tasks, agreeing even when uncomfortable, and suppressing personal opinions to avoid conflict. The concept of minorities being naturally submissive is problematic.

However, code-switching requires altering one's speech, demeanor, or appearance to conform to the dominant culture's expectations. While these behaviors may appear as effective short-term solutions, they ultimately negatively impact one's mental and emotional health. The effort of constantly masking a person's true identity can lead to burnout and even a crisis of confidence, as individuals are left wondering if their success is truly theirs or a result of their conformity due to trauma.

Janelle's story captures this struggle vividly. She spent years accommodating her colleagues' expectations, shrinking herself to fit a mold that exhausted her. Fortunately, she recognized the need for boundaries and self-assurance, which led to a turning point in her journey. Instead of accepting extra tasks without question or letting her ideas be dismissed, Janelle began to say "no" to unreasonable demands and to speak up when her contributions were overlooked. She learned to claim her space and voice professionally, which positively affected her personal life. This shift didn't come easily; it required her to let go of the generational fear of being labeled as the stereotypical "angry Black woman." Yet, it was precisely this reclaiming of agency that allowed her to challenge the unspoken rules of her workplace. Boundaries and assertiveness became her tools for survival and empowerment, enabling her to exist authentically while also advocating for systemic change.

The journey toward developing boundaries and assertiveness is not just about individual empowerment; it also has the potential to inspire broader cultural shifts. For workplaces truly looking to become inclusive, minority employees should feel that their authentic selves are valued. Organizations must understand that relying on employees to adapt and fit into a pre-existing, often exclusionary culture is not sustainable or fair. Instead, workplaces must foster an environment that actively seeks out and respects diverse voices. This begins with a culture that allows employees to say "no" without repercussions, acknowledges and strengthens interpersonal communication skills that encourage constructive feedback loops and empathy, and holds everyone accountable for maintaining an inclusive environment that values all minorities and their lived experiences.

However, achieving this level of inclusion requires more than superficial DEI efforts. Many companies implement DEI initiatives that look good on paper but do little to address structural inequities. Workshops on implicit bias, while informative, often fail to create lasting change if they do not lead to concrete actions and policy adjustments. The story of Janelle emphasizes this inadequacy: the DEI sessions at her company were performative, a way for management to check a box without examining or altering the systemic norms that upheld discrimination and exclusion. True progress demands a shift from a performative allyship to an active allyship, which involves sustained efforts to understand and dismantle the power structures that disadvantage minority employees.

To drive real change, organizations must take actionable steps that go beyond one-time training sessions. First, they should engage in a thorough audit of their policies and practices, identifying areas where bias and inequity are embedded. This might include revising hiring practices to reduce the impact of unconscious bias or ensuring that performance evaluations are based on measurable outcomes rather than subjective criteria that can be influenced by stereotypes. Additionally, companies should create accountability mechanisms, such as regular assessments of workplace culture and anonymous feedback channels where employees can safely voice concerns.

Moreover, leaders must model inclusive behavior, demonstrating vulnerability and openness to learning from their mistakes. This might involve leaders sharing their own experiences with bias or engaging directly in difficult conversations about race and equity. Organizations should invest in long-term mentorship programs that actively support and uplift minority employees. These programs should focus on breaking down the barriers to advancement that often exist for minorities and providing opportunities for leadership development.

It's not enough to simply ask minorities to adjust when systematic racism and white supremacy have long shaped workplace practices. While survival tactics such as people-pleasing and code-switching provide temporary protection, they also suppress genuine identities and perpetuate injustice. When people like Janelle establish boundaries, declare their value, and reclaim their proper space, real transformation starts.

However, change is not solely the responsibility of marginalized individuals. Instead of superficial DEI efforts, organizations need to commit to deep, systemic change by eliminating bias, demanding accountability from everyone, and building a culture where real inclusion flourishes. Then, and only then, will we be able to eliminate the unspoken rules that have dominated corporate culture for far too long, paving the way for a future where every voice is heard, valued, and respected.

BIO

Shakira Releford is an Associate Professor in Social & Behavioral Sciences. Her expertise comes from 12 years of experience as a behavior analyst, mental health professional in recovery, trauma-informed specialist, and educator. Her personal experience living with OCD has motivated her to take control of her life and share her lived experience as an entrepreneur, facilitator, and trauma-informed yoga teacher to inspire others to reduce their anxiety and fulfill their purpose-driven life. Shakira founded the 501(c)(3) nonprofit, Connecting Youth Achievement Center, to provide social-emotional and educational support to Black and Indigenous youth with neurodivergence in marginalized communities. Shakira uses positive intelligence and biblical teachings to help change people's lives. She works as a consultant for neurodivergent business owners and charitable organizations.

Connect with Shakira on LinkedIn at www.linkedin.com/in/shakira-releford.

4

Navigating Leadership: Career Transitions and Growth

Leila Lawson

THE WEIGHT OF REPRESENTATION

I n 2004, Kansas City found itself at a pivotal point, torn between its past and future. While the city demonstrated its conservative stance by joining other states in banning same-sex marriages, many residents actively pushed for better civil rights protections and fairer social policies. This tension manifested in ongoing racial inequality issues. Despite progress since the Civil Rights era, the city still grappled with apparent racial divides; Black and minority residents had less access to quality housing, faced more barriers to good education, and had fewer job opportunities compared to non-minority residents.

BREAKING INTO LEADERSHIP

In my mid-twenties, I secured my first leadership position as a local marketing manager while working part-time at an airline for flight benefits. The management position came with a nice pay increase from my previous role. Excitedly, I phoned my best friend in L.A. to share the news.

"Girl, guess what?" I blurted out before she could answer, sharing what felt like a huge success.

"I'm so happy for you, girl; you deserve it!" she responded. We had been friends since sixth grade, and I knew if anyone would celebrate with me, even from afar, it would be her. She shared advice from her corporate experiences, and I eagerly listened as she detailed both the benefits and challenges of management.

The position offered me the opportunity to hire and train employees and make a difference. However, being the youngest person, the only female, and the only minority in the office, the weight of representation rested heavily on my shoulders. Still, I felt a sense of accomplishment as I began my new career and enjoyed my new vehicle. Growing up, my dad drove Cadillacs for as long as I could remember. So, as one could imagine, owning a Cadillac Escalade as an adult reminded me of my childhood and the good times I spent riding with my father.

At 25, I felt proud of my achievements, unaware that my success would highlight the ongoing challenges of navigating a world still affected by discrimination. One day, after completing an inventory count, I drove to Walmart. As I exited my vehicle, a male voice called out.

"Is this your car?" he asked, referring to the Escalade.

"Yes," I replied, slightly confused.

"Really, how's someone like you able to get a car like that?"

"I have good credit and pay my bills on time," I responded sharply. This interaction was my first encounter with what I would later learn was called a microaggression—a term coined by Dr. Chester M. Pierce of Harvard University in the 1970s to describe insults and dismissals non-Black Americans often inflicted on African Americans ("Microaggressions" n.d.).

As I navigated my new role, I quickly learned that the playing field was far from level. Through an accidental revelation during a team meeting, I discovered I was significantly underpaid compared to my peers doing the same job. After two years of dedicated work fostering partnerships and generating revenue, I requested a meeting with the company president to renegotiate my salary. His dismissive response that "my bonuses should suffice" was disappointing but not entirely surprising.

When I later requested a cost-of-living raise, the company president suggested I could "find elsewhere to work" if I wasn't satisfied with my pay. Soon after advocating for myself, my position became precarious. I faced increased micromanagement and additional tasks my peers didn't have to complete. Each time I raised concerns about this treatment, I received vague responses until finally, my manager simply stated, "It's just not working out."

Though demoralizing, this experience taught me valuable lessons. I realized that in an inherently biased system, working hard wasn't enough; I needed to be strategic, document my achievements, and seek out allies and mentors who could advocate for me. As the only woman and person of color in leadership, I understood that my journey wasn't just about me; my experiences would likely impact opportunities for others like me.

Rather than continue in an environment that undervalued my contributions, I decided to forge my own path. While maintaining my part-time airline position as a gate agent, I launched my own business selling essential oils. I realized I could channel my effort into building something for myself rather than a company that didn't recognize my worth.

The key lesson I learned was simple but powerful: seize opportunities by pursuing your natural passions and stand up for yourself, even in the face of challenges. If you enjoy educating people on a specific topic, become a subject matter expert through courses and research. Create your own opportunities, whether through teaching or content creation, and don't let others define your worth.

CONFRONTING BIAS IN EVERYDAY LIFE

The Walmart parking lot incident was just the beginning. A few years later, while driving my Escalade, I was pulled over by a police officer who asked, "Whose car are you driving?"

Mine," I responded firmly. The officer claimed the vehicle was reported stolen, but after checking my license and insurance, he backtracked, saying there had been a mistake. Though I felt targeted, I had no way to prove it at the time.

These experiences echoed the early lessons of my life. Having lost my mother at age nine, I learned about life's unfairness early. My grandmother, grounded in faith, always advised me to take the higher road and turn the other cheek. She emphasized the importance of hard work, even if it meant working multiple jobs; advice that shaped my entire approach to life.

During the 2008 recession, as businesses collapsed and employees faced furloughs, I began considering more stable employment options. While working my airline job, a police sergeant repeatedly suggested I consider becoming an officer. Initially, I dismissed the idea; my only interactions with law enforcement had been receiving speeding tickets as a teenager, and I had no desire to be viewed as "the enemy." The sergeant persisted, noting my strong interpersonal skills with airline customers and suggesting I could make positive changes from within the system.

Despite my family's skepticism, I applied and was accepted to the police academy. It was there that I discovered a disturbing truth. I overheard officers discussing how they would "get creative" to pull vehicles over, with one openly admitting, "Yeah, we would tell people that their vehicle came back as stolen to get them to stop and identify everyone in the car." This revelation hit home; I had been a victim of this exact discriminatory practice. Instead of deterring me, it strengthened my resolve to ensure fair and respectful treatment for all citizens.

However, speaking up for equality proved more challenging than I anticipated. In both the academy and later in my career, my questioning of certain practices and suggestions for more equitable approaches often met resistance. During meetings, when I raised concerns about problematic practices, colleagues would either fall silent or dismiss my input, labeling me as "angry" or "uptight." Some suggested that highlighting potential biases undermined department unity rather than promoting necessary change.

The personal cost of confronting workplace bias was significant. Work relationships became strained, career advancement opportunities diminished, and the environment grew increasingly hostile. For months, I questioned whether speaking up was worth the backlash, whether it would have been easier to "go along to get along."

But each time I considered staying silent, I remembered my own experience during that traffic stop, the helplessness and frustration. I thought about others facing similar treatment if these practices went unchallenged. My position within the system provided a unique opportunity to effect change from the inside, and with that opportunity came responsibility.

I learned to be strategic in my advocacy, choosing battles carefully, framing concerns constructively, and building alliances with like-minded colleagues. Though my commitment to fair treatment and work-life balance sometimes set me apart, each small victory; whether a policy revision, a shift in colleague perspective, or more respectful citizen treatment; reinforced the value of persistent advocacy.

This journey has taught me that confronting bias requires more than occasional acts of courage; it demands continuous commitment to justice and equality. It calls for resilience, strategic thinking, and unwavering belief in the possibility of change. While the path of an advocate can be lonely and frustrating, it's essential for creating a truly equitable society.

The lesson is clear: Personal biases exist, but meaningful change starts with open, candid communication. When building relationships or understanding others, we must move beyond assumptions and verbal cues to engage in honest dialogue. Only through such authentic exchanges can we begin to dismantle the biases that persist in our everyday lives and institutions.

RISING ABOVE AND PAVING THE WAY

Rather than letting discrimination and bias discourage me, these challenges fueled my determination. I refused to let others' prejudices define my path or limit my potential. Instead, I channeled my experiences into creating positive change from within the system.

My resilience stemmed from a deep-rooted spiritual foundation. Raised in the church and taught to put God first, I drew strength from my faith throughout my journey. While this spiritual connection didn't exempt me from discouragement, it provided the courage and conviction to push through moments of doubt. Each setback revealed itself as a setup for the next level in life.

This faith-based perspective became my anchor, helping me view every challenge as an opportunity for growth. I understood that my purpose extended beyond immediate circumstances, which prevented me from remaining in a place of defeat. This mindset proved essential as I continued my professional development, eventually becoming a licensed professional life coach; a role that enhanced my leadership abilities and allowed me to support others on their journeys.

A pivotal moment came with my ADHD diagnosis. What initially seemed like another obstacle transformed into a breakthrough, offering new insights into my cognitive processes. This understanding enabled me to develop strategies that worked with, rather than against, my unique thinking style. More importantly, it deepened my empathy for others facing hidden challenges and strengthened my commitment to creating truly inclusive environments.

As a police officer, I leveraged these varied experiences, as a woman of color, a person of faith, a professional with ADHD, and a leader in a male-dominated field, to champion diversity and inclusion initiatives. I actively sought mentorship opportunities, both as a mentee and mentor, particularly focusing on supporting young professionals from underrepresented backgrounds. This involved navigating complex office politics while maintaining my values and consistently addressing microaggressions and unfair practices.

In my community work, I initiated crucial conversations about unconscious bias and pushed for improved employee morale. I created safe spaces for colleagues to share their experiences and collectively develop solutions. My role as a life coach complemented these efforts, allowing me to empower others facing similar challenges. By openly sharing my story, including both struggles and triumphs; I helped clients recognize their strengths and advocate for themselves effectively.

Rising above personal challenges became more than individual success; it was about paving the way for others. Each time I spoke up in meetings, challenged biased assumptions, or mentored emerging professionals, I recognized that my actions contributed to creating a more inclusive environment for future generations. During moments of isolation or doubt, I drew strength from my faith, purpose, and the knowledge that others were counting on me to persevere.

This journey taught me that rising above is a continuous process of growth and advocacy. It requires:

- Turning challenges into opportunities for positive change
- Using personal experiences to drive systemic improvements
- Staying true to core values while adapting to new circumstances
- Working actively to dismantle barriers rather than just overcoming them
- Lifting others while climbing

My ongoing mission extends beyond personal achievement to creating a world where everyone, regardless of their background, neurodiversity, or personal challenges, has the opportunity to thrive. This commitment manifests through several key principles:

First, self-advocacy is non-negotiable. Speaking up about unfair treatment and negotiating for deserved recognition sets important precedents. When traditional paths prove blocked, creativity and networking can forge new routes forward. Building a strong support network of mentors and allies provides crucial guidance and encouragement.

Second, continuous education serves as a powerful tool for empowerment. Understanding your rights and industry standards strengthens your position and ability to effect change. As you advance, using your position to advocate for systemic changes becomes both a responsibility and an opportunity.

Finally, maintaining integrity through adversity ensures that success comes on your own terms. Perseverance, while challenging, ultimately validates the belief that positive change is possible through sustained effort and unwavering commitment to one's principles.

This journey has shown me that true leadership isn't just about personal advancement, It's about creating lasting positive change that benefits everyone. By staying grounded in faith, embracing our unique characteristics, and maintaining a commitment to justice, we can transform workplace challenges into opportunities for growth and systemic improvement.

A CALL TO ACTION

Reflecting on my journey, from a 25-year-old navigating a challenging work environment to my current leadership position; I'm struck by the dual power of perseverance and representation. To those who find themselves facing similar challenges today: your presence matters, your voice matters, and your success creates ripples that extend far beyond your immediate circumstances.

To allies and leaders in positions of influence: I challenge you to examine your biases and the systems within your organizations with clear eyes and honest hearts. Ask yourself:

1. Are you providing truly equal opportunities and support to all employees?
2. Does your workplace merely tolerate diversity, or does it actively celebrate and nurture it?
3. Are you actively working to dismantle barriers that hold back talented individuals from underrepresented groups?

The path to genuine diversity and inclusion stretches before us, long and demanding. Yet each step forward, each policy changed, each voice amplified, each barrier removed; brings us closer to a world where success stems from merit and potential, not from race, gender, or background. Let us commit to being the change we wish to see, transforming our workplaces and communities through deliberate decisions and conscious actions, day by day.

Remember: your journey transcends personal success. You are laying foundation stones for those who will follow in your footsteps. Stand tall, speak your truth, and never underestimate the profound impact of your presence and voice. Together, through unwavering commitment and courageous action, we can create a more diverse, inclusive, and equitable world for generations to come.

Explore my book, *Successfully Diverse: A Guide for Diverse Professionals in Leadership*, for further insights on embracing diversity and fostering a healthy work-life balance. In it, I delve deeper into strategies and practices that inspire change and empowerment for everyone, everywhere.

And remember: "In a world full of replicas, find the leader within yourself." —Gottabeme79

BIO

Leila is a certified professional life coach with Gottabeme79 Leadership and Training. She guides clients through personal and career transitions, combining evidence-based coaching techniques with a compassionate, client-centered approach. Her expertise spans effective communication, work-life balance, and self-confidence building, empowering clients to create meaningful changes in their lives.

Her 15-year law enforcement career includes service as an airport operations specialist, K-12 instructor for D.A.R.E. and G.R.E.A.T. programs, youth crisis intervention trainer, and sergeant with the Kansas City Missouri Police Department. Prior to law enforcement, she worked in marketing, where she developed promotional policies, managed trade show operations, and conducted strategic data analysis.

With a Bachelor of Arts in Communications, Leila brings a unique blend of law enforcement insight, marketing acumen, and coaching expertise to her practice, offering clients a holistic approach to personal and professional development.

Connect with Leila on LinkedIn at www.linkedin.com/in/gotta-beme-leila-lawson.

5

Journey Through Loss and Identity

Dr. Mary Darden-Robinson

I was raised in a loving and adventurous military household, moving from one country and base to another, which allowed me to immerse myself in diverse cultures and opportunities. However, at the age of eight, my life was profoundly disrupted by the loss of my father. This event transformed me from a happy, charismatic little girl who adored her dad into a confused and unsettled child, ultimately evolving into a rebellious young woman desperately seeking a sense of belonging.

The loss of my father altered the course of my life in ways I could not fully comprehend at the time. My mother and grandparents worked tirelessly to provide stability amidst the chaos, but their efforts were met with challenges as I began to rebel. Initially, my rebellion seemed to be an attempt to numb the overwhelming emotions for which I had no coping mechanisms. As my mother set boundaries, I eagerly tested them. While she sought to guide me toward becoming a sensible and polite young lady, I resisted out of curiosity and a longing for independence. The life she envisioned for me was filled with opportunities, yet it inadvertently limited my ability to learn essential life lessons through my own experiences.

One pivotal experience occurred during my time at a prestigious private school, where I was one of the few Black children in a predominantly privileged environment filled with the children of local doctors and lawyers. Initially, my peers were kind and welcoming, but I soon felt the weight of my difference. Instead of embracing my background, I found myself feeling increasingly isolated. Despite these challenges, my mother insisted I remain at the school, believing that this experience would academically prepare me for success. When I eventually transitioned back to public school, I felt like a stranger, struggling to connect with peers whose experiences were starkly different from mine.

As graduation approached, I could hear my father's voice echoing in my mind: "Mary, go to college, get an education." As his devoted daughter, I set my sights on this goal with determination.

In college, I excelled academically and maintained a low profile. However, I gradually discovered my authentic self. I enjoyed expressing my individuality through long colored nails and dyed hair. While this self-expression brought me joy, there were moments when I felt compelled to code-switch and adhere to more socially acceptable standards, behaving in ways that reflected my upbringing—well-to-do and proper.

Yet, as time passed, I realized that no matter how I presented myself—even when conforming to societal expectations—I faced criticism. I vividly remember a moment in a public speaking class when my professor remarked, "I'm sorry I couldn't hear anything you said because I was distracted by your nails." This experience underscored a harsh reality: people will scrutinize my choices whether or not I try to fit in. I came to the realization that I should embrace my true self, as I would be judged no matter what.

INTRODUCTION TO BARRIERS IN THE WORKPLACE

In the pursuit of professional advancement, particularly for women of color, the journey is often fraught with systemic challenges that manifest in various forms. This chapter examines four significant barriers that impact the authentic expression and success of African American women in the workplace. I call these phenomena: The Place Holder, Diversity Deserts, The Mascot, and Hijacking/Ghostwriting.

The Place Holder phenomenon highlights the disheartening reality of being perceived as a mere token in the workplace. As a Black woman navigating the mental health and substance use industry, I have experienced the anxiety and frustration of awaiting decisions regarding my worth, only to be told that I was not doing enough to warrant a pay increase. This dismissive assessment felt like a clear signal that my contributions were undervalued and that my voice was unwelcome in critical discussions.

Despite my responsibilities in assessing program impacts and developing essential documentation, I found myself relegated to the sidelines, struggling to prove my worth in an environment that seemed intent on keeping me from the table. This experience often left me feeling like a pawn in a larger game, where my feedback was ignored, and my achievements went unrecognized. I began to realize that my interviews for new roles were often mere formalities, designed to fulfill a legal obligation rather than a genuine interest in my qualifications. This cycle of being overlooked became a painful pattern, prompting me to create a blacklist of organizations that perpetuated this phenomenon.

The Diversity-Desert Workplace further compounds these challenges. Despite my educational accomplishments, including a Doctorate in Psychology, I found myself in environments that professed to value diversity but failed to embody it in practice. The disconnect between verbal commitments to inclusivity and the reality of workplace culture often left me feeling isolated and undervalued. It is crucial to recognize that a workplace may appear diverse on the surface, yet true inclusivity is reflected in the actions and behaviors of its leaders. Empty slogans about diversity do little to combat the microaggressions and inequities experienced daily.

The Mascot barrier describes the struggle of being perceived as a token representative of diversity rather than a valued contributor. My vibrant personality and unique style often seemed to serve as a showpiece for a diversity-friendly workplace, but my qualifications were typically an afterthought. The pressure to conform to outdated ideals of professionalism often clashed with my authentic self, creating a difficult tension between self-expression and career advancement.

Lastly, Hijacking and the expectation of Ghostwriting without recognition represent another pervasive issue in professional dynamics. I have repeatedly encountered situations where my contributions were stripped of recognition, with my name omitted from documents I had diligently produced. This practice not only undermines individual contributions but also stifles professional growth and visibility, leaving employees feeling marginalized and exploited (Darden-Robinson 2024).

MAINTAINING WELL-BEING AND NAVIGATING HOSTILE WORKPLACES

Encountering systemic barriers and hostile workplace dynamics, prioritizing well-being is not just essential—it's a form of resistance and a path to thriving against the odds. Despite being overlooked, underestimated, and even undermined, I've learned to use these strategies to not only protect my peace but also excel in my career. Below are practical steps I've relied on to safeguard my mental, emotional, and professional health, helping me to flourish even in environments that were not designed for my success:

Strategies for Maintaining Well-being

1. **Build a Support Network** - Cultivate relationships with mentors, peers, and professional groups who understand your experiences and can provide guidance, encouragement, and advocacy. Consider joining organizations specifically focused on empowering women of color in the workplace.

2. **Set Boundaries** - Clearly define and communicate your boundaries at work. Protect your time, energy, and mental health by saying "no" to unreasonable demands and tasks that devalue your contributions.

3. **Seek Professional Help** - If workplace challenges impact your mental health, consider speaking with a therapist or counselor, preferably someone familiar with intersectional issues. Therapy can provide coping strategies and a safe space to process your experiences.

4. **Celebrate Small Wins** - Acknowledge and celebrate your accomplishments, no matter how small. Keeping a personal record of achievements can remind you of your value when it feels overlooked by others.

5. **Practice Self-Care** - Engage in activities that replenish your energy and foster resilience, such as exercise, meditation, journaling, or spending time with loved ones. Make self-care a non-negotiable part of your routine.

6. **Focus on Growth** - Identify areas for personal and professional growth that align with your long-term goals. Use workplace challenges as opportunities to sharpen your skills, network, and enhance your portfolio, even if the recognition isn't immediate.

Strategies for Hostile Environments

1. **Document Everything** - Maintain a detailed record of incidents, including dates, times, and participants. If you experience discrimination or harassment, having documentation can strengthen your case when reporting internally or externally.

2. **Leverage Resources** - Research and utilize internal resources like employee assistance programs (EAPs), diversity officers, or ombudspersons. If these resources are lacking, consider external support from legal counsel or advocacy groups.

3. **Explore New Opportunities** - If the environment is toxic and unchangeable, prioritize finding a new position in an organization that aligns with your values. Treat the transition as an investment in your long-term happiness and growth.

4. **Stay Aligned with Your Values** - Resist the urge to internalize hostility or change your identity to fit oppressive norms. Stay authentic and seek spaces where you are valued for who you are and what you bring to the table.

5. **Report Hostile Practices** - If you feel safe doing so, report hostile behaviors through official channels within the organization. Ensure your report is framed professionally and backed by documentation.

6. **Exit Gracefully** - If the situation becomes untenable, develop an exit strategy. Focus on building connections, saving funds, and securing opportunities before making your departure. Leaving on your terms can help you reclaim your agency.

Strategies to Affect Change from Within

1. **Raise Awareness** - Organize workshops or seminars within organizations to educate employees about the barriers faced by women of color. Share personal stories and case studies that highlight these challenges to foster empathy and understanding.

2. **Create Safer Spaces** - Establish support groups or mentorship programs specifically for women of color, allowing them to share their experiences and strategies for overcoming barriers. Encourage open dialogues about diversity and inclusion in team meetings and organizational forums.

3. **Advocate for Policy Changes** - Collaborate with leadership to review and revise workplace policies that may inadvertently perpetuate inequality, such as hiring practices, promotion criteria, and pay structures. Propose the implementation of diversity training programs that focus on unconscious bias and inclusive leadership.

4. **Promote Representation** - Encourage organizations to actively seek diverse candidates for leadership positions and create pathways for their advancement. Highlight the importance of diverse perspectives in decision-making processes and project teams.

5. **Implement Feedback Mechanism** - Establish anonymous channels for employees to provide feedback on their experiences related to diversity and inclusion in the workplace. Use this feedback to inform ongoing training and policy adjustments.

6. **Recognize and Celebrate Diversity** - Create initiatives that celebrate the contributions and achievements of women of color within the organization. Host events that showcase diverse cultures and perspectives, fostering a sense of belonging and appreciation.

7. **Encourage Accountability** - Develop metrics to measure the effectiveness of diversity and inclusion initiatives, holding leadership accountable for progress. Regularly review these metrics and share the outcomes with the entire organization to maintain transparency.

8. **Support External Organizations** - Partner with external organizations that focus on empowering women of color in the workplace, providing resources and networking opportunities. Encourage employees to participate in community outreach programs that promote diversity and inclusion beyond the organization.

9. **Foster Lifelong Learning** - Promote continuous education on topics related to diversity, equity, and inclusion through workshops, webinars, and reading groups. Encourage employees to stay informed about best practices and emerging trends in inclusive workplace strategies.

10. **Lead by Example** - Encourage leaders and managers to model inclusive behavior, actively seeking input from diverse team members and valuing their contributions. Share your own commitment to diversity and inclusion, demonstrating the importance of these values in your leadership style.

As I reflect on my journey, I am reminded of the resilience that has carried me through loss, identity struggles, and professional barriers. Each challenge I faced has shaped the person I am today—a person who thrives not despite adversity, but because of the lessons it has taught me.

BIO

Dr. Mary Darden-Robinson is a dedicated director, licensed therapist, speaker, trainer, and consultant with over 20 years of experience in mental health and substance use services in Hampton Roads, VA. In her directorial role, she oversees program development and implementation, ensuring that services effectively promote overall wellness. Utilizing an eclectic approach that integrates Cognitive Behavioral Therapy (CBT) and Motivational Interviewing (MI), she enhances client outcomes and fosters a supportive environment.

As a director, she leads initiatives aimed at serving underserved populations across various settings, including residential and community programs. She is committed to creating a culture of excellence and collaboration among her team, providing clinical supervision and mentoring emerging professionals in the field. In her capacity as a speaker and trainer, she empowers others to address mental health and substance use challenges. Additionally, as a consultant, she offers strategic insights to organizations seeking to improve their service delivery and community impact.

Dr. Darden-Robinson is also a co-author of *Triumph in the Trenches: Navigating Success for Black Professionals*, where she provides valuable insights into career advancement and professional development. She holds multiple certifications, including Licensed

Professional Counselor (LPC), Substance Abuse Treatment Practitioner (LSATP), and Certified Substance Abuse Counselor (CSAC). She earned her bachelor's degree in human services counseling from Old Dominion University, a Master's in Community Counseling from Norfolk State University, and a Doctor of Psychology from Walden University.

Connect with Dr. Mary on LinkedIn to explore her impactful leadership, training, and consulting contributions in the mental health field.

6

The Invisible Battle: Navigating the Minefield of Workplace Accommodation

Rev. Dr. Xenia Barnes

magine a bustling corporate office, its walls adorned with vibrant posters proclaiming, 'Diversity is Our Strength' and 'Inclusion for All.' The air buzzes with the energy of a thousand conversations, punctuated by the rhythmic tapping of keyboards and the occasional burst of laughter from a nearby meeting room. At first glance, it is a tableau of modern workplace harmony. However, beneath this carefully curated surface, there lies a stark contrast. This seemingly inclusive environment is a landscape fraught with invisible barriers and unspoken struggles. In this sea of supposed inclusivity, individuals with physical, mental, and sensory disabilities often find themselves adrift, their unique needs lost in the chorus of well-meaning but ultimately hollow proclamations.

In recent years, organizations worldwide have embraced the clarion call for diversity and inclusion with a fervor that borders on the evangelical. Corporate mission statements overflow with promises of equality while HR departments roll out initiative after initiative to create a more inclusive workforce. The intentions behind these efforts are genuine, and the enthusiasm is palpable.

Yet, as we peel back the layers of these diverse drives, we uncover a sobering truth: good intentions alone are not enough. For many individuals with disabilities, the much-vaunted push for inclusion has unintended consequences. It has become a double-edged sword that promises acceptance with one hand while inadvertently erecting new barriers with the other. This reality challenges our assumptions about true inclusion and forces us to confront the often-vast gulf between intention and impact in the modern workplace.

Consider the case of Sarah, a brilliant software engineer with high-functioning autism. Her company, a tech giant known for its progressive policies, proudly touts its commitment to neurodiversity. However, Sarah is drowning in a sea of open-plan offices, mandatory team-building exercises, and "flexible" work hours that wreak havoc on her need for routine. While well-meaning, the company's one-size-fits-all approach to inclusion fails to account for the nuanced needs of neurodivergent individuals like Sarah (Szuic et al. 2021).

This scenario is not unique. Across industries, blanket policies are implemented to create an inclusive environment. However, these policies often fall short, creating a paradoxical situation where attempts at inclusion lead to exclusion. As Roberson, Ryan, and Ragins note in their comprehensive study of workplace inclusion practices, "Standardized inclusion policies, while appearing equitable on paper, can inadvertently marginalize the very individuals they aim to support" (Roberson et al. 2017).

The crux of the issue lies in the failure to recognize that true inclusion requires individualization. It demands a willingness to adapt and flex, not just on the part of the employee with a disability but on the part of the organization. Nevertheless, as we will explore throughout this chapter, many companies remain stubbornly wedded to the idea that a single policy can address the diverse needs of all employees.

IN WRITING, PLEASE: THE SILENT SCREAM OF THE ACCOMMODATION SEEKER

The process of requesting workplace accommodation is akin to navigating a bureaucratic minefield. What should be a straightforward process of identifying needs and implementing solutions often devolves into a Kafkaesque nightmare of paperwork, delays, and subtle (or not-so-subtle) discouragement.

As a trauma coach and leader of multiple gun violence survivor groups, I have encountered countless parents returning to work after the murder of a loved one or even their child. A grieving mom and gun violence survivor with PTSD who works in a high-functioning city agency shared the overwhelming stress of being surrounded by forced joy in the workplace. When she requested a quieter workspace to help manage her symptoms, she was met with a barrage of forms, each more intrusive than the last. "It felt like I was being put on trial," the mother recalls. "Every request was met with skepticism as if I was trying to game the system rather than simply do my job effectively. Being forced to sit among individuals consistently celebrating birthdays, office baby showers, their children's accomplishments, continuously being asked to smile or partake in small talk, and unnecessary meetings that trigger emotional breakdowns. I was drowning in a balance that had no regard for my mental well-being."

Gun violence affects a staggering portion of the population. Fifty-nine percent of adults, or someone they know or care about, have experienced gun violence in their lifetime. This number is even more alarming within specific communities: Seventy-one percent of Black adults, 60 percent of Latinx adults, and 58 percent of white adults or someone they know or care about have experienced gun violence in their lifetimes. These statistics reveal the widespread impact of this trauma and underscore the urgent need for workplace policies that accommodate survivors' mental health needs, rather than compounding their distress with bureaucratic hurdles and skepticism ("Gun Violence Survivors in America," n.d.).

Unfortunately, this experience is far from uncommon. Chang and Aaronson found that 68 percent of employees with disabilities reported feeling discouraged or intimidated by the accommodation request process (Chang and Aaronson 2023. The same study identified several common tactics used by companies to delay or deny accommodation requests:

- Offering alternative solutions that do not address the core need

- Questioning the necessity of the accommodation
- Citing undue hardship without proper evaluation
- Excessive documentation requirements
- Prolonged "review" periods

These tactics amount to what can only be described as corporate gaslighting—a subtle but pervasive form of discrimination that leaves employees questioning their own needs and rights. As noted by Cho, "The accommodation process often becomes a war of attrition. Companies bank on the fact that many employees will give up rather than continue to fight an uphill battle" (Cho 2022).

THE COMPETENCE CONUNDRUM

In the modern workplace, there exists a troubling disconnect between physical presence and actual competence, a gap that disproportionately affects individuals with disabilities. This phenomenon, which we might call the "competence conundrum," manifests in the persistent belief that being seen equates to being productive.

For many employees with invisible disabilities, this creates an untenable situation. They find themselves caught between the need to manage their condition and the pressure to conform to outdated notions of productivity. As Garcia and Thompson point out in their groundbreaking study on workplace productivity metrics, "Traditional measures of employee engagement and productivity often fail to capture the unique contributions of neurodivergent individuals or those with non-apparent disabilities" (Garcia and Thompson 2024).

Michelle's psychological safety has continuously changed due to executives' desire to have all staff work in the office—her long-lasting PSTD and unwavering triggers of depression are met with barriers of repetitive requests for doctor notes and requests for in-person meetings. Despite consistently delivering high-quality work and meeting all deadlines, Michelle faced constant scrutiny from management due to her need for flexible hours and unlimited remote work-from-home days. The company's rigid adherence to "face time" as a measure of dedication completely overlooked her output and value to the team.

This disconnect between presence and performance is not just a matter of individual frustration; it has far-reaching implications for organizational success. A recent meta-analysis by Yoon, Choi, and Suh found that companies with flexible work policies focusing on output rather than hours logged reported higher overall productivity and employee satisfaction (Yoon et al. 2022). Yet, many organizations cling to outdated notions of what "work" looks like to the detriment of employees and the bottom line.

THE EMPATHY GAP: WHY YOUR STRUGGLE IS NOT MY STRUGGLE

One of the most persistent challenges in creating truly inclusive workplaces is bridging the empathy gap between individuals with and without disabilities. This gap often does not arise from malice but rather from a lack of understanding and an inability to fully grasp experiences beyond one's own. Rodriguez, a leading researcher in organizational psychology, describes this phenomenon as "experiential myopia"—the tendency to assume that one's own experiences are universal or easily understood by others (Chen 2024).

THE HIDDEN COST OF CONFORMITY: WHEN ADAPTATION BECOMES SELF-BETRAYAL

For many individuals with disabilities, particularly those with invisible or neurodevelopmental conditions, the workplace becomes a stage where they must constantly perform a version of "normalcy" that aligns with neurotypical expectations. This phenomenon, known as "masking" or "camouflaging," comes at a significant personal cost.

Taylor, a neurodiversity advocate and organizational psychologist, describes masking as "a survival strategy that allows individuals to navigate a world not designed for them, but at the expense of their authentic selves" (Taylor 2023). The pressure to conform to neurotypical norms can lead to burnout, increased anxiety, and a profound sense of disconnection from one's true identity.

Consider the experience of Emma, a talented graphic designer with autism. In her quest to fit in with her neurotypical colleagues, Emma spends enormous energy suppressing stimming behaviors, forcing eye contact, and engaging in small talk that she finds both confusing and exhausting. Emma is physically tired and emotionally drained from constant performance by the end of each workday.

The idea that conformity equals success is deeply ingrained in many corporate cultures. However, this notion is increasingly being challenged by research showing the benefits of neurodiversity in the workplace. A groundbreaking study by Ling, Sato, and Brown found that teams with neurodivergent members demonstrated higher levels of creativity, problem-solving ability, and innovation than homogeneous neurotypical teams (Ling et al. 2022).

REWRITING THE RULES: TOWARDS A TRULY INCLUSIVE WORKPLACE

It is time to move beyond lip service. Hope is no longer enough; today, there is no room for a divide. All workplaces must be efficiently held accountable for crafting a culture of genuine acceptance. As we have explored throughout this chapter, the path to true workplace inclusion for individuals with disabilities is fraught with challenges. However, it is crucial to move beyond critique and towards actionable solutions. Creating an authentically inclusive environment requires a fundamental shift in organizational culture, policies, and practices. If you are wondering what you can do as a leader to move the needle forward, you are already on the right path, as seen in this chapter. I have included some actionable and critical steps to support allies of the movement for true inclusion and equity of visible and invisible disabilities like mine and those you have read about thus far.

Here are some critical steps organizations can take to move toward true inclusion:

1. **Individualized Accommodation Processes**: Replace rigid, one-size-fits-all accommodation policies with flexible, individualized approaches. This might involve creating a dedicated team trained in disability rights and accommodation best practices.

2. **Education and Awareness Training**: Implement comprehensive training programs for all employees to increase their understanding of diverse disabilities and working styles. These programs should go beyond basic sensitivity training and include practical strategies for creating inclusive team dynamics.

3. **Redesign of Physical and Digital Spaces**: Adopt universal design principles in physical office spaces and digital tools to ensure accessibility for all employees, regardless of ability.

4. **Flexible Work Policies**: Embrace truly flexible work arrangements focusing on output and results rather than physical presence or rigid schedules.

5. **Neurodiversity-Affirming Recruitment and Retention Strategies**: Develop hiring practices that recognize and value neurodivergent talents and create career development paths that accommodate diverse working styles.

6. **Regular Inclusivity Audits**: Conduct regular assessments of workplace culture, policies, and practices to identify and address barriers to inclusion.

The benefits of embracing neurodiversity and varied abilities in the workplace are well-documented. A comprehensive study by

Wong and Silverman found that companies with solid disability inclusion practices reported 28 percent higher revenue, 30 percent higher economic profit margins, and twice the net income of companies that did not prioritize disability inclusion (Wong and Silverman 2024).

Moreover, creating a genuinely inclusive environment benefits all employees, not just those with disabilities. As noted by Patel in his recent work on organizational psychology, "When we design workplaces that accommodate diverse needs and working styles, we create an environment where everyone can thrive" (Patel 2023).

The journey toward genuine workplace inclusion for individuals with disabilities is ongoing and multifaceted. It requires constant reflection, adaptation, and a willingness to challenge deeply ingrained assumptions about work, productivity, and success. By embracing all employees' unique strengths and perspectives, organizations can create more inclusive workplaces that are innovative, productive, and humane workplaces.

THE HIDDEN STRUGGLE: BLACK WOMEN, MENTAL HEALTH, AND WORKPLACE INEQUALITY

Yes, laws may have been put in place, but they have not truly protected all women in the workplace. Black women, in particular, have been generationally conditioned to hide their mental health conditions and needs behind a mask called resilience. For Black women, there is no place at work for feelings, imperfections, or margins of error due to mental health conditions—we must work twice as hard as our peers—and more than three times as hard as white men—just to be considered part of the so-called 'pool of potential.' The data confirms this stark reality. Studies show that only 30 percent of Black employees feel comfortable requesting mental health accommodations compared to 45 percent of white employees (McKinsey & Company 2023). Black women are 2.3 times less likely to receive requested workplace accommodations when they do ask (Society for Human Resource Management, 2023).

The compounding impact of domestic violence on workplace performance creates additional barriers; 83 percent of Black women experiencing domestic violence report workplace performance impacts, and 55 percent report job loss related to abuse situations (National Partnership for Women & Families 2022). It should not surprise but enrage us that the toll on mental health is severe; Black women experiencing domestic violence are three times more likely to develop PTSD (American Journal of Public Health 2022). Recent studies have established that 64 percent report anxiety/depression linked to community gun violence exposure (Urban Institute 2023).

These statistics tell only part of the story. Behind each number is a woman struggling against systemic barriers while being expected to maintain an image of unshakable strength. The "strong Black woman" stereotype continues to mask very real pain and deny access to needed support and accommodation in the workplace. The question is, "What are we going to do about it?"

CHARTING THE PATH TO TRUE INCLUSION

As we navigate the complexities of creating truly inclusive workplaces, we must hold onto hope and envision a future where individuals with disabilities can thrive without barriers. Imagine a workplace where diversity is not just celebrated in posters and policies but woven into the very fabric of daily operations. In this ideal environment, requesting reasonable accommodations is as natural and stress-free as asking for office supplies. Picture a world where managers are trained to recognize and support diverse needs, flexible work arrangements are the norm rather than the exception, and success is measured by output and innovation rather than hours logged or physical presence. This workplace is where neurodiversity is seen as a strength, assistive technologies are readily available, and open dialogues about mental health are encouraged without stigma.

While the path to this ideal may be challenging, it is far from impossible. By fostering a culture of empathy, continuously educating ourselves and others, and reimagining our processes with inclusivity at their core, we can create workplaces where every individual, regardless of their abilities or disabilities, can bring their whole selves to work and contribute to their fullest potential. This is not just a dream but an achievable reality that benefits not only individuals with disabilities but entire organizations and society as a whole.

As we reflect on the challenges and opportunities discussed in this chapter, let us consider seven key takeaways that can guide our path forward:

1. **Individualization is Key**: One-size-fits-all policies often fail to address the diverse needs of employees with disabilities. True inclusion requires flexible, personalized approaches to accommodation.

2. **Invisible Disabilities Matter**: Not all disabilities are visible. Organizations must cultivate awareness and understanding of invisible disabilities to create truly inclusive environments.

3. **Challenge Assumptions**: Many workplace norms and expectations are built on neurotypical assumptions. Questioning and reimagining these norms is crucial for fostering inclusion.

4. **Empower Through Education**: Ongoing education and awareness training for all employees is essential in bridging the empathy gap and creating a culture of understanding.

5. **Embrace Flexibility**: The ability to adapt quickly to changing needs and circumstances is a hallmark of genuinely inclusive organizations.

6. **Value Diverse Perspectives**: Neurodiversity and varied abilities bring unique strengths and insights. Embracing these differences can drive innovation and success.

7. **Continuous Improvement**: Creating an inclusive workplace is not a one-time effort but an ongoing learning, adapting, and improving process.

The choice is clear. Choose to create a workplace where everyone's unique strengths are recognized, valued, and empowered. In doing so, we enhance our organizations and enrich our society. By choosing a path of inclusion, organizations create workplaces where all employees can thrive, regardless of their abilities or disabilities. They choose to see every individual's full potential and create environments where that potential can be realized. The path to true inclusion may be challenging but infinitely rewarding. As we move forward, let us remember that every step towards greater understanding, every policy adapted, and every assumption challenged brings us closer to a world where all individuals can fully participate and contribute in the workplace.

BIO

Xenia Barnes leverages behavioral analysis and community activism experience as a dynamic speaker, author, and trauma coach transforming domestic abuse, gun violence, and illness survivors. As a PhD candidate, her acclaimed talk inspires audiences on loving themselves through trauma. Her coaching polishes inner gems so teams can enhance performance via strategic thinking, smart management, efficient planning, and essential training.

Visit Xenia at www.xeniabarnes.com.

7

The Audacity to Thrive: Triumph Over Toxicity

Glynnis Swan

The *audacity* to expect a sense of belonging, psychological safety, recognition and credit, advocacy, allyship, accountability, and the freedom to lead authentically—without the fear of being micromanaged, tokenized, isolated, culturally conditioned, pressured to overperform, or labeled angry or aggressive in the workplace. Yet, for many black professionals, these fundamental expectations remain unmet, often eclipsed by the pervasive shadow of toxic leadership. Toxic or abrasive leadership isn't just an unfortunate byproduct of corporate culture—it's a systemic issue, leaving us uniquely vulnerable to its most damaging impacts. The intersection of racial bias, exclusion, and abrasive leadership creates a perfect storm that not only stifles careers but erodes mental well-being, innovation, and trust.

Laura Crawshaw, acclaimed Boss Whisperer,™ defines an abrasive leader as "any individual charged with managerial authority whose interpersonal behavior causes emotional distress in coworkers sufficient to disrupt organizational functioning" (Crawshaw 2023).

This behavior can include excessive micromanagement, public humiliation, gaslighting, and outright bullying, which foster environments of fear, stress, and diminished productivity. Abrasive leaders often prioritize results over relationships, leaving deep psychological and professional scars on those they manage.

As a Black female professional with over two decades of corporate experience, I've endured my share of discrimination, harassment, gaslighting, exclusion, micromanagement, humiliation, bullying, and retaliation from various leaders. However, it wasn't until I worked with one particular leader—let's call them Jordan—that I experienced all of these behaviors in just six months.

Though Jordan and I were expected to collaborate almost daily to ensure project success, our interactions were anything but collaborative. Jordan refused to meet with me one-on-one, disparaged me in front of clients, undermined my authority with my team, excluded me from critical meetings and decisions, and deliberately provided false or inaccurate information to jeopardize my employment and compensation.

Even before our initial meeting, Jordan questioned my leadership capabilities and worthiness. They even asked a colleague, "Can she even write an email?" The blatant disregard and hostility I faced were not just professional challenges; they became deeply personal assaults on my competence, integrity, and identity.

In one of my final contentious conversations with Jordan, they asked for feedback on their communication style. I responded candidly, describing it as condescending and dictatorial. Flushed and fumbling for words, Jordan erupted, shouting: "In my entire career, I have never been spoken to this way!" I calmly replied, "Well, maybe if somebody had, you wouldn't be sitting here talking crazy to me today."

Admittedly, not my finest moment. But after months of enduring Jordan's constant jeering, microaggressions, and outright disrespect with professionalism, tact, and diplomacy—and with no support from senior leadership or HR—I reached my limit. I stood up to the bully in a language they could understand, and for the first time, Jordan was silent; there was no grimace, sarcasm, or dismissive response.

Those months were the worst of my professional career. Toxicity saturated my workspace, and Jordan thrived in it, grinning and reveling in their dominance, often exclaiming, "I love it when I get my way." The stress was all-consuming. The mere thought of interacting with Jordan triggered nausea, migraines, and body pain so severe that some days, I couldn't get out of bed. I masked the toll with heavy concealer and false lashes to hide my swollen eyes, but the stress betrayed me—I couldn't eat, couldn't concentrate, and even started losing my hair. The anxiety of potentially losing my job loomed constantly, and I found myself lashing out at loved ones, projecting the frustration and helplessness I felt in the workplace. Worse, I doubted my abilities, questioned my worth, and grew bitter toward the organization that enabled this toxic behavior.

During that conversation, I reached a breaking point: It was me or Jordan, and I chose me. I blended empathy with assertiveness and made it clear that their behavior was unacceptable. That pivotal moment sparked a shift in me. It marked the beginning of my self-advocacy journey, one in which I held leaders accountable and highlighted the organizational costs of allowing toxicity to fester.

I began implementing coping strategies (which I'll share later) to reclaim my peace and move beyond merely surviving to thriving. I also realized that many toxic leaders are oblivious to their abrasiveness. That insight led me to reflect on my own leadership, questioning whether gaps might exist between how I perceive myself and how others experience me.

This chapter aims to empower professionals of color to recognize, navigate, and overcome the challenges posed by toxic leadership. By exploring its psychological roots, impact on teams and individuals, and offering practical strategies for resilience and advocacy, I will equip professionals to persist and prevail in environments that often feel stacked against them. Additionally, I will highlight actionable steps leaders can take to combat toxic workplaces and foster cultures of inclusivity and respect.

THE PSYCHOLOGY OF TOXIC LEADERSHIP

Toxic leadership isn't born in a vacuum. It stems from a mix of personal insecurities, systemic enablers, and organizational cultures that inadvertently reward or tolerate destructive behaviors. Understanding the psychological roots of these behaviors can illuminate why toxic leaders consistently undermine their teams and why organizations often struggle to address the issue effectively.

Traits and Behaviors of Toxic Leaders

Abrasive leaders consistently exhibit behaviors that create emotional distress, disrupt team cohesion, and erode trust. While their tactics may differ, the following traits are commonly observed:

- Narcissism: Toxic leaders often center themselves, viewing their team as extensions of their ego rather than collaborators. They deflect accountability with statements like, "Why don't you like me?" or "This team is so dramatic."

- Gaslighting: Manipulating others to question their perceptions, such as dismissing legitimate concerns with, "You're overreacting," or invalidating experiences of bias or mistreatment.

- Micromanagement: A compulsive need to control every aspect of a team's work signals a deep insecurity about relinquishing power.

- Belittling Comments: Statements like, "I can't believe we're paying these people to do this," reveal a disregard for the value and contributions of their team.

In the 2024 article, "The Importance of Empathy in the Workplace", Dr. Crawshaw highlights a broader range of toxic behaviors, including:

Shouting	Hitting people
Swearing	Making threats

Name-calling	Being dismissive
Discrimination	Throwing/Hitting objects
Ignoring, excluding	Maligning another's character or reputation
Storming out of meetings	Sarcasm: hostile humor, public humiliation
Intimidation: e.g. glaring, snorting	Sexual comments or behavior

These behaviors often thrive in corporate environments that tolerate unchecked power dynamics, lack robust accountability mechanisms, and prioritize results over relationships, creating fertile ground for toxicity.

1. Insecurity and Power Dynamics - At the heart of many toxic behaviors lies insecurity. Leaders lacking confidence in their abilities often compensate by exerting dominance and control. This can manifest in micromanagement, public criticism, or a refusal to delegate tasks. They mask their perceived inadequacies in attempting to assert power over their team. Power dynamics exacerbate the issue. Leaders in hierarchical structures, bolstered by positional authority, often view dissent or constructive feedback as challenges to their status rather than growth opportunities.

2. Lack of Empathy - Empathy is a cornerstone of effective leadership. Studies from organizations like the Center for Creative Leadership consistently demonstrate that empathetic leaders foster collaboration, engagement, and high performance (Center for Creative Leadership 2024). In contrast, leaders who lack empathy struggle to connect with their teams, misinterpret feedback, and often prioritize results over relationships. This lack of empathy can result in dismissive behaviors, such as ignoring the impact of toxic comments or failing to address concerns about workplace culture. These leaders may justify their approach with statements like, "I'm here to get the job done, not to mess with all the touchy-feely stuff."

3. Cognitive Biases - Toxic leaders are often shaped by cognitive biases that distort their perceptions and decision-making:

- Halo Effect: Favoring specific individuals while unfairly scrutinizing others, creating an inequitable work environment that fosters resentment.

- Confirmation Bias: The tendency to seek out information that supports preconceived notions, such as assuming a team member is incompetent and only noticing their mistakes while ignoring their successes.

- Fundamental Attribution Error: Overemphasizing personal flaws to explain others' failures while attributing their own mistakes to external factors. For example, a toxic leader might blame an employee's "lack of commitment" for a missed deadline while excusing their own poor planning.

4. Common Assumptions about Abrasive Leaders - It is a common misconception that toxic leaders are fully aware of the nature and impact of their abrasive behaviors, act with malicious intent, or are incapable of change. However, research from the Boss Whisperer Institute reveals that:

- Most toxic leaders are unaware of how their behaviors affect others; they are often oblivious.
- Their intent is typically not evil; they believe they are "doing what it takes to get the job done."
- Many abrasive leaders can change their behaviors through proper coaching and intervention [Lovett 2023]

Additional contributors to chronic patterns of abrasive behavior include:

- Cultural Norms: What might be perceived as acceptable behavior in one culture may be viewed as abrasive in another.
- Family Interactive Styles: Growing up in environments where harsh or abrasive styles were normalized can shape an individual's leadership approach.
- Directness vs. Abrasiveness: Some leaders mistakenly believe being direct excuses their abrasive behavior, saying things like, "I don't believe in sugar-coating things."
- Lack of Training: Without training in conflict resolution or emotional intelligence, individuals may default to aggressive, abrasive approaches, resorting to a "fight" response when challenged.

5. The Ripple Effect: Team Dynamics and Toxic Leadership - Consider these striking statistics:

- **56%** of employees report experiencing toxic leadership during their careers (Hogan Assessments 2023).
- Toxic cultures are **10.4** times more likely to drive attrition than compensation concerns (Sull et al. 2022).
- Black employees are **2–3** times more likely to experience workplace microaggressions than their white peers (Society for Human Resource Management 2024).

Toxic leadership doesn't operate in isolation—it reverberates across teams, eroding morale, shattering trust, and stifling productivity. While the immediate victims bear the brunt of the harm, the ripple effects weaken team cohesion, stifle innovation, and sabotage organizational performance.

For professionals of color, the stakes are even higher. Systemic inequities, compounded by racial bias, microaggressions, and exclusion, intensify the damage. Black and underrepresented employees, often among the few in their workplace, face heightened exposure to targeted behaviors and limited avenues for support.

Toxic leadership isn't just a moral failing—it's a strategic and financial risk. Organizations that fail to address it suffer from decreased morale, diminished productivity, and costly turnover. Tackling toxic leadership is non-negotiable for companies committed to fostering inclusion and retaining diverse talent.

6. Decreased Morale and Productivity - Toxic leaders can devastate team morale. They prioritize power, control, or results at any cost, creating environments rife with fear, tension, and disengagement. Microaggressions and exclusionary practices further alienate marginalized team members, who often expend significant energy navigating these dynamics instead of focusing on their work.

For professionals of color, cultural gaslighting—where leaders dismiss or invalidate experiences of bias—exacerbates feelings of isolation and reduces their sense of belonging. Over time, this toxic environment drains motivation, reduces creativity, and suppresses the diverse perspectives essential for innovation.

7. Increased Turnover - Teams with toxic leaders often experience high turnover. Employees subjected to disrespect, micromanagement, or public humiliation seek refuge elsewhere, leading to a costly cycle of hiring and retraining. For professionals of color, the revolving door is even faster. The additional burden of navigating bias and exclusion in a toxic environment accelerates burnout, causing many to leave not just their role but their organization entirely.

8. Erosion of Trust - Trust is the foundation of any successful team. Toxic leadership erodes this foundation, creating an environment where team members feel unsupported, undervalued, and uncertain of their place. Leaders who engage in gaslighting, favoritism, or punitive measures foster mistrust among team members and between the team and leadership.

Professionals of color often face the brunt of this erosion, as they may feel particularly vulnerable to unequal treatment or retaliation when speaking up. This lack of trust ripples outward, diminishing collaboration, productivity, and the psychological safety necessary for teams to thrive.

9. The Toll of Mental Health - Toxic leadership can devastate mental health, manifesting as chronic stress, anxiety, and depression. The constant fear of unpredictable behavior, unfair treatment, or public humiliation creates an environment of hypervigilance, where employees feel perpetually on edge, unable to relax or focus. Over time, this persistent stress erodes mental and physical well-being, resulting in a range of harmful symptoms.

Physical symptoms often include headaches, muscle tension, digestive issues, fatigue, and a weakened immune system, making individuals more susceptible to illness (American Psychological Association 2013). Psychologically, toxic leadership can lead to difficulty concentrating, irritability, mood swings, insomnia, and social withdrawal (Gandolfi 2022). These effects are not temporary; when sustained over long periods, they can develop into severe conditions like post-traumatic stress disorder (PTSD) or other long-term psychological trauma.

PTSD is a condition more commonly associated with extreme trauma but is increasingly recognized in workplace contexts (Stergiopoulos et al. 2011). According to the National Health Service, symptoms of PTSD may include:

- Hypervigilance: Feeling perpetually on edge or fearing future harm.
- Nightmares: Experiencing recurring dreams about traumatic incidents.

- Avoidance: Steering clear of situations, people, or tasks that evoke trauma memories.
- Flashbacks: Reliving distressing workplace events, such as public humiliation or targeted hostility.
- Emotional Numbness: Experiencing detachment from emotions makes connecting with others difficult.

In addition to PTSD, toxic leadership significantly contributes to burnout—a state of emotional, physical, and mental exhaustion caused by prolonged stress. Employees subjected to undervaluation, micromanagement, and inadequate support often disengage, feeling powerless and unmotivated. Burnout symptoms include chronic fatigue, cynicism, decreased productivity, and an increased likelihood of absenteeism ("The Psychological Effects of Micromanagement," n.d.). Left unaddressed, it can result in severe mental health challenges and drive talented professionals out of the workforce entirely.

For professionals of color, the impact of toxic leadership is often compounded by systemic inequities, such as discrimination, microaggressions, and exclusion. These overlapping challenges intensify the psychological toll, creating a uniquely hostile environment. Furthermore, in many communities of color, the stigma surrounding mental health often discourages individuals from seeking help (Mass General Brigham McLean 2022). The cultural emphasis on resilience and self-reliance can lead to internalized shame and silence, preventing professionals from accessing therapy or other support systems that could aid recovery. Addressing this stigma is crucial. By normalizing conversations about mental health within these communities and advocating for culturally competent resources, organizations and leaders can help dismantle these barriers.

Why Managers Enable Toxic Leaders

American employers lose a staggering $777.9 billion due to employee disengagement, with an additional $136.8 billion directly attributable to turnover tied to workplace injustices—totaling over $917 billion as the cost of toxic workplaces ("The State of Workplace Injustice Report a Fact Sheet of Workplace Injustice in America," n.d.).

While toxic leaders are responsible for their behavior, managers and organizations often enable their destructiveness, whether intentionally or inadvertently. Key factors contributing to this pattern include:

- Systemic Bias: Professionals of color, particularly Black employees, frequently face higher thresholds to validate their concerns. Their feedback is often dismissed as oversensitivity or misinterpreted as cultural misunderstandings.

- Focus on Results: Organizations prioritizing short-term performance metrics over long-term well-being often reward toxic leaders who "deliver results" at the expense of team morale and cohesion.

- Conflict Avoidance: Many managers avoid addressing toxic behavior out of fear of confrontation, disruption, losing a high-performing individual, or personal repercussions.

- Lack of Accountability: Weak performance review systems and a reluctance to investigate employee complaints create environments where toxic behaviors persist unchecked.

Organizational leaders often fail to recognize that managing conduct is as critical as managing performance and make common mistakes such as:

- Lacking the skills or tools to address abrasive behavior effectively.
- Relying solely on factual evidence while dismissing negative perceptions.
- Assuming people cannot change and viewing termination as the only solution.

A CALL FOR ACTION

To combat toxic leadership, organizations must take proactive measures:

1. Implement transparent feedback mechanisms: Encourage anonymous feedback and act on concerns swiftly and fairly.
2. Ensure leadership accountability: Hold leaders to behavioral standards, prioritizing team well-being and psychological safety.
3. Prioritize inclusion over egos: Cultivate a culture where collaboration, empathy, and respect are rewarded.

Leaders must also confront their reluctance to intervene by considering the following questions:

1. Can the organization afford to overlook these perceptions while maintaining its values and goals?

2. Are the negative perceptions of this behavior creating barriers to organizational success and performance?

3. Would I accept this behavior if it were directed at someone I care about, such as a family member or close friend?

4. How does continuing to be perceived negatively serve the abrasive leader's long-term interests or career growth?

5. Does this conduct align with my personal and professional standards, even if it doesn't meet the formal definition of bullying?

The Path to Resolution - Understanding the psychology of toxic leadership is the first step in dismantling its impact. For organizations, this means holding leaders accountable for results and team health, cohesion, and retention. For individuals, it requires developing strategies to navigate these dynamics and advocating for systemic change.

When businesses embrace empathetic, inclusive leadership as a necessity rather than a luxury, they pave the way for healthier workplaces. These environments allow all professionals—particularly those from marginalized backgrounds—to thrive, unlocking the full workforce potential.

Strategies for Coping and Thriving - My experiences with toxic leadership taught me that prayer and reflection provide solace, but genuine thriving requires actionable strategies. The following five approaches are designed to mitigate the negative impacts of toxic leadership and empower you to take control of your well-being and career:

1. Set Boundaries Intentionally, Communicate them Clearly, and Enforce them Unapologetically - Boundaries are your first line of defense against toxic behavior. Begin by assessing your situation: What boundaries am I neglecting, and what do I need to reclaim my peace? Use clear "I" statements to express your needs without blame. For example, say, "I need uninterrupted time to complete my tasks effectively," rather than focusing on the leader's faults.

- Minimize Unnecessary Contact: Focus on essential interactions and avoid unproductive engagements.
- Protect Work-Life Balance: Turn off work notifications after hours and resist bringing work-related stress home.
- Seek Common Ground: Finding areas of agreement can foster rapport and reduce tension, even in difficult relationships.
- Choose Your Battles: Address critical issues strategically, conserving emotional energy.

2. Build a Support Network - Toxic environments can isolate you, making a strong support system essential.

- Mentors and Coaches: Seek guidance tailored to your career and personal goals.
- Colleagues: Share your experiences with trusted coworkers who can offer solidarity and advice.

- Therapists: Professional counseling can help you process the emotional toll and build resilience.

Seeking help is a sign of strength, not weakness. Prioritizing your mental health is critical for long-term success.

3. Prioritize and Practice Self-Care - Your well-being must take precedence, even in challenging circumstances.

- Reflect weekly on which self-care actions to prioritize to sustain your health and happiness.
- Maintain physical health through adequate sleep, balanced nutrition, and regular exercise.
- Incorporate mindfulness or meditation to manage stress and maintain focus.
- Engage in enjoyable activities—spending time with loved ones, pursuing hobbies, or exploring creative outlets.

Self-care is not indulgence; sustaining your professional and personal strength is necessary.

4. Document Incidents of Toxic Behavior - Documentation provides leverage to address or escalate toxic situations effectively.

- Keep Detailed Records: Note dates, times, and specifics of problematic behaviors.
- Preserve Evidence: Save emails, texts, and other communications that exemplify toxicity.
- Consult Experts: Engage HR or legal professionals to understand your options.

- Prepare for Escalation: Act only when you feel ready, weighing risks and benefits.

When the environment becomes intolerable, prioritize your health and professional growth over enduring further harm.

5. Develop an Exit Strategy - Sometimes, leaving a toxic environment is the most empowering step you can take.

- Evaluate Alternatives: Consider transferring to another team or seeking opportunities outside the organization.
- Leverage Your Network: Explore new roles through referrals and connections.
- Polish Your Professional Brand: Update your resume and LinkedIn profile to highlight your skills and accomplishments.
- Research and Prepare: Align your next opportunity with your values and career aspirations.

Exiting a toxic workplace isn't giving up—it's reclaiming your mental health and career trajectory.

Building Resilience and Leading Authentically - Addressing toxic leadership requires more than policies and procedures—it demands a cultural transformation where every employee, regardless of background, can thrive. Leadership training, cultural audits, and robust accountability mechanisms are essential, but actual progress comes from a commitment to fostering environments where advocacy, equity, and accountability are not exceptions but norms.

For professionals of color, this means creating workplaces that amplify voices, validate concerns, and hold toxic leaders accountable for the harm they cause. Confronting toxic leadership is not just about protecting teams; it's about unlocking the full potential of a diverse and empowered workforce.

Fostering Resilience and Self-Preservation - Resilience isn't merely about enduring adversity—it's about thriving, learning, and maintaining authenticity despite challenges.

To navigate toxic environments while preserving well-being:

- Cultivate Emotional Agility: Develop the capacity to adapt to stress and change without losing your sense of self.

- Anchor in Core Values: Use your principles as a compass to guide decisions and maintain focus in difficult situations.

- Prioritize Self-Care: Protect your mental and physical health through boundaries, support networks, and recognizing when to step away.

Avoiding the Perpetuation of Toxic Traits - Nearly everyone displays abrasive behavior at some point in their career. Authentic leadership demands self-reflection and a commitment to growth:

- Empathy: Build trust by understanding and respecting diverse perspectives, especially those of marginalized team members.

- Self-Awareness: Regularly evaluate your leadership style. Seek feedback to uncover and address blind spots.

- Integrity and Accountability: Hold yourself to high standards, acknowledge mistakes, and strive to improve.

Leadership also requires the courage to act. Intervene when toxicity arises, ensuring your actions foster an inclusive, respectful environment.

Display Accountability - Accountability goes beyond addressing issues—it ensures sustained change:

- Verify progress through open dialogue and follow-ups.
- Check-in with team members who raised concerns, asking, "How are things now?"
- Reward positive change but enforce consequences for persistent toxicity.

Empower Through Advocacy - Resilience transcends individual survival; it is a catalyst for systemic change. Advocacy and allyship are potent drivers of healthier, more inclusive workplaces.

Build Supportive Networks

- Mentorship: Seek and offer guidance to navigate challenges, foster confidence, and build resilience.
- Amplify Voices: Advocate for peers whose concerns may be dismissed or minimized, ensuring their perspectives are heard and validated.
- Collaborate for Change: Unite with colleagues to champion equity, psychological safety, and inclusive organizational practices.

Advocate for Systemic Change

- Leadership Role Models: Remind executive leaders that their behavior sets the tone for organizational culture. By modeling empathy, integrity, and inclusivity, they create a standard that cascades throughout the organization.

- Training and Development: Provide managers with tools to address toxicity, such as conflict resolution, emotional intelligence, and implicit bias training.
- Cultural Audits and Transparency: Regularly evaluate organizational norms to identify and address areas of toxicity. Transparent decision-making fosters trust and reduces perceptions of favoritism or inequity.
- Accountability Mechanisms: Establish and enforce clear policies that include zero tolerance for toxic behaviors. Swift, consistent actions demonstrate that such conduct is unacceptable and reinforce a culture of accountability.

By prioritizing advocacy, leaders can transform resilience from a coping mechanism into a force for meaningful and lasting change, creating environments where employees feel supported, valued, and empowered to thrive.

SUMMARY

Toxic leadership isn't just a personal failing—it's a systemic issue with profound consequences for individuals, organizations, and society. This chapter has delved into the devastating effects of toxic leadership on morale, productivity, and culture, with a particular emphasis on its amplified impact on professionals of color. Yet, amidst these challenges lies the potential for transformation through accountability, resilience, and collective action.

Toxic leadership comes with a steep price with complacency resulting in:

- Eroding Morale: 26% of employees dread going to work (Society for Human Resource Management 2019).

- Financial Losses: $223 billion in turnover costs due to bad company culture over the past five years (Society for Human Resource Management 2019).

- Employee Exodus: 68% of female professionals have encountered toxic workplaces, with more than half leaving their roles (MIT Sloan Management Review 2023).

- Reputational Damage: High-profile cases from Amazon, Uber, and Facebook showcase the fallout of unchecked toxic behaviors, leading to lost trust and diminished growth (Robinson 2024).

Organizations that ignore these dynamics gamble with their bottom line, workplace culture, and reputation. They must prioritize fostering cultures of psychological safety where employees feel valued and respected. Every leader has the capacity to learn, grow, and foster cultures that inspire, not destroy. Implement 360-degree feedback systems and leadership development programs and address underlying toxicity drivers. Leadership accountability isn't optional— it's essential for building workplaces where everyone can thrive.

To my Black professionals, toxic leadership does not define you. Your power lies in your ability to overcome, advocate, and transform. Together, we can demand better leadership, foster collective action, and create workplaces that empower everyone to succeed.

BIO

Glynnis is an award-winning executive coach, career strategist, and conflict intervention specialist who inspires ambition, action, and accountability. Her mission is to empower Black and Brown professionals to overcome corporate obstacles, elevate their careers, and thrive in inclusive workplaces.

A credentialed Global HR professional, mediator, and trauma-informed coach, Glynnis brings over two decades of transformative expertise. Her career spans corporate consulting and HR leadership roles at industry giants such as EY, Deloitte, Xerox, and Microsoft. Glynnis is a passionate advocate for social justice, using her platform to champion equitable workplace cultures.

Known for her ability to address challenges head-on, Glynnis specializes in coaching abrasive leaders to reframe negative perceptions and build emotionally intelligent leadership practices. Her work transforms conflict into collaboration, mediocrity into excellence, and potential into performance.

Connect with Glynnis and learn more by visiting her website, edgeofaudacity.my.canva.site/coach.

8

Aboagye

Dr. Sherone Smith-Sanchez

In the Akan language, Aboagye means "One who is powerful and complete"–a fitting description for those who engage in the struggle for social justice (MyloFamily 2018). As you may know, social justice work is exhausting, traumatic, and requires the unwavering support of both colleagues of color and allies. The fight is skewed and can be better illuminated through my story of a warrior woman named Aboagye.

Imagine with me in this saga, a young girl barely taller than a preschooler. Visualize the beads of sweat as they bubble down Aboagye's sun-scalded cheeks. Squinting at her opponent, her heart races. She curls and uncurls her sweaty fists, shifting her weight from side to side, and panting like Bolt, after his third world record in a single Olympic Game. Amid the crowd's chants of "FIGHT! FIGHT!" She hears a girl safely behind her state the obvious: "No sah. This fight is not fair!" She is correct. This opponent is twice Aboagye's size and three years older than her. Aboagye sizes her up and knows instinctively that she must strike while her nemesis distractedly sneers, and snarls. So, WHUP...She hits her opponent with all she has and keeps going till she is declared the winner. Like Aboagye, this is how many social justice warriors in the American workforce survive work, and life in general. We fight bullies.

Like Aboagye's opponent, systems of oppression are pervasive in our society despite it being more than six decades past Dr. Martin Luther King's famous "I have a dream" speech. We remain woefully dependent upon imbalanced systems of professional advancements 110 years after Marcus Mosiah Garvey formed the UNIA!

What is our recourse, when our economic standing appears minimal and as tiny as Aboagye? How can we fight a system of oppression, much like Aboagye's opponent that seems much older and larger than our efforts to gain economic parity? We fight the bully. As a black professional woman in the USA I, and many of you, fight work bullies now in a similar heated struggle.

GOOD TROUBLE NEEDS GOOD COMPANY

Like many, my arsenal of warrior weapons includes love, patience, coaching sessions, policy revisions, endless clarifying emails, grant writing, and unity. More than anything we fight fear. The struggle is no less strenuous or fairer than Aboagye's primary school Friday Fights. Similar to her situation, the fights are extremely unfair and others who could support the persecuted colleague in unfair work environments watch from a safe distance as their colleague struggles through conflicts regarding micro-aggression, salary parity, sexism, hairstyles, viewpoints, and unfair promotion practices. They comment occasionally on how rough it must be. They see that the fight isn't fair, but most watch from a seemingly safe distance, just as their ancestors watched 400+ years of dehumanization in the form of slavery and colonization. The few cheerleaders yelling, "FIGHT! FIGHT!" give much needed validation and strength to the social justice warrior.

Institutional racism and dehumanization, two primary demonic tools of slavery and colonialism, have created social weaponry that is so embedded in organizational policies and practices that many colleagues cannot see a problem and are afraid to do so. Consequently, some sneer at terms such as BLM, DEI, LGBTQ, BIPOC and 'Woke Culture', while others wonder why peers can't just align themselves with the policies and be fine. So, work-bullying and discrimination are difficult to navigate because the punches are invisible.

This is what makes social justice struggles so traumatizing and exhausting. It is also what necessitates that we create a sense of community as we grow and learn another way to exist. The Black professional needs allies and colleagues who support them in speaking truth to power. Good trouble needs good company. When we overlook social justice-related issues that we think don't directly affect us, we unintentionally escalate inequity and help to define a space that has repercussions for the entire workforce down the road.

This unfair work culture issue can permeate all aspects of society, including religious organizations. I experienced this dynamic personally, as I have concurrently worked as part of leadership teams in church organizations, supporting lead pastors while functioning as leadership in secular positions. For me, issues of social injustice in both arenas are starkly similar. Sundays at numerous houses of worship, the place where many should find solace, and healthy, family-like relationships, often hold their own similar challenges.

Why? As spiritual leaders, we too, can battle unconscious systems of institutional racism and varied forms of oppression in church-settings which are simply microcosms of society. It's been my experience, after 35 years as clergy, that many American church organizations tend to stick to the societal paths similar to the secular world. Those systems created unhealthy competition and mimicked a pecking order that once pitted house slave against field slave, evolving into structures that leave the diaspora vying for limited resources between groups within organizations.

One vehicle giving longevity to this issue is theophobia, an irrational and persistent fear of God, religion, or the divine, which was a tool used to control the colonized and enslaved in the African Diaspora. Theophobia did not teach reverence of a loving God. Instead, it taught first an irrational fear of God's wrath and secondly an unhealthy fear of the oppressor as a representative of this vengeful God. These ideas have stolen their way into both our secular and religious circles where engendering fear is often misunderstood as a healthy sign of organizational leadership. These ideas about leadership are a part of the genesis of organizational bullying and discrimination, evidenced strongly in secular and ministerial arenas.

These grave leadership errors leave many church organizations living still, not under grace, but as though we are under the bondage of fear, reading and living by the old Slave Bible (1807). This game is hidden in plain sight and is designed to keep us moving along on treadmills meant to imitate growth and perpetuate myths of the absolute infallibility of clergy.

The flipside of that game is the imposter-ship of some who do not truly believe in the lie of their own leadership superiority. Oddly enough, both sides of this coin are rooted in fear, the very opposite of the faith that should guide our work. It is therefore my belief, that consequently, historically, many in church leadership have created titles and niches that have nothing to do with the gospel and everything to do with elevating ourselves. Therefore, the competitive, backbiting spirit that isolates those deemed different lurks among many professionals and affects the church leaders' work culture also. This is dark, harmful stuff, from which we need deliverance beloved, as it often deters us from being the societal salt and light.

Like secular environments, anyone who deviates from accepted patterns of behavior in many church environments ruled by Theophobia are not always lovingly corrected. Sometimes, to emphasize negative repercussions of being different they are made an example of by the misguided leader, and publicly, verbally flogged. During my tenure in one particular church organization, I was not exempt and frequently heard phrases from the pulpit such as: "You are not special. God don't care if you a doctor!" All eyes would glance in my direction as I was often the only doctor in the room. My quiet, confident demeanor did not change. I am called to be an Empress, and part of a Royal Priesthood. Theophobia does not reign in this delivered mind and body. Instead, I responded by lovingly establishing appropriate boundaries and committing to studying and understanding the venom.

I learned in both spaces that leadership meetings can become strange dances with the Black female leader working to convey respect and pressing on to be productive while dodging thinly veiled racist and misogynistic efforts to keep her in a contrived place. I have watched sadly as people exited potentially wonderful spiritual homes and told me they were uncomfortable and disappointed with these behaviors that impeded their spiritual growth. My story indicates that social justice work belongs in and by the religious organizations also.

The work is wearying and can be as stressful as work in secular realms. It requires the willingness to fight, interspersed with moments of purposeful respite and reflection, mixed liberally with the unwavering support of colleagues, congregants of color and allies. Most importantly, it requires a journey away from legalism and theophobia to embrace the love that I urge us in both secular and spiritual circles to share. These are all part of the weaponry. We cannot run, we must, like Aboagye, figure out how to fight. Why? Our ability to thrive as individuals and as a nation depends upon this. We owe it to the ancestors who lost their lives, and the children who have not yet begun theirs.

THE WAY FORWARD

In my church leadership circumstance, I employed the weaponry of prayer, love, and refusal to cower in fear, as we pressed our way through this thing without a name. Finally, during a much-needed talk at what felt like a very unholy leadership retreat, I learned that the strange public insults were less about a personal attack, and more about a Black leader's fear of not pleasing God, as they battled imposter syndrome. The willingness to have difficult discussions is a vital tool in our fight to escape the grip of institutionalized forms of racism and bias.

The term imposter syndrome was created by Dr. Pauline Clance and Dr. Suzanne Imes to describe fictional feelings of unworthiness and inadequacy. This is often the culprit in unhealthy competitiveness among leaders of color that occurs in many organizations where people vie for coveted roles. In recovering quickly from the jolt of this revelation, I did the only thing I could. I expressed love and forgiveness; first, for the sake of my mental and spiritual health; and secondly, to give my co-leaders assurance. Love can be a phenomenal weapon. When we use love, we fight behaviors, not people.

As Black leaders, we must understand the genesis of what we believe to be behavior meant to harm us. It is larger than us. The way forward is forgiveness through the difficult conversations where we name and cast out that devil. In our talk, I conveyed my love and forgiveness, that I was comfortable in my own skin as a leader and Black Jamaican American woman and had no ambitions to conduct a coup to take over their pulpit or congregation. We continued to establish healthy communication boundaries and lavishly offered each other love. Those were hard conversations, and I wish I could say we worked through it immediately. However, iron does not sharpen iron overnight. I believe that our pressing on took us past the subsequent escalated persecution which took on ridiculous levels.

Why did I not exit as others had done, and why should you consider whether you need to stand up to bullies in the same way that Aboagye did? My response is in a message I preached one Sunday titled "Soldier, STAY on your post!" in which I emphasized my belief that the living God places us in environments where we can learn and grow together. I emphasized then and stress now that if the environment is toxic to the point where you are losing yourself and your mind, you should immediately transition to a healing space. Return to the battlefield when you feel healthy, balanced, and restored. Every battlefield does not suit every warrior. We must first determine if in fact, that is our post, then do the work to understand each other and come out of cycles of institutionalized insanity, whole.

As has been done for me, we all have been gifted with the possibility of a focus that remains on love, respect, and unity. I have learned that my inner peace does not come from people, a pose, or a prose. It comes from the quiet conversations that I have in prayer and the still, small, response I get when I hear: "Keep going. Keep growing. They know not what they do. Keep loving." This is the kind of love that gets reciprocated at church or any institution. Unwavering faith and unconditional love are not for the fainthearted. They are the

111

weapons that help us to fight by speaking truth to power even when it attempts to make us afraid.

ABOAGYE, HOW WILL WE FIGHT?

As we look inward, let's select the right weaponry. Societally, we have tried self-flagellation: an educational system that favors leniency for groups merely on the basis of skin color and economic standing and a legal system steeped in institutionalized racism that punishes our Black sons for being Black and terrorizes whole groups of people for their skin tone, beliefs, and sexual orientation.

America is NOT the 'Land of the Free' for everyone. Some are free-er than others. It is therefore time for us to recognize and remove these radical toxicities from our homes, organizations, our work environments, our churches and other places of worship. So how DO we fight like Aboagye? This acronym FIGHT will help you to compile your weaponry while you strategically select your battles: FEAR NOT. We must resolve to be fearless in our collective pursuit of deeper levels of equity, inclusion, and respect, as we forge ahead with unwavering conviction. When overwhelming panic, anger, anxiety, and a host of other emotional and mental responses set in, retreat, breathe, and remind yourself that you are not alone. There are millions of Aboagyes (social justice warriors) with you. Some of us have teamed up to convey our love and support of you through the pages of this book.

Inspire change through your consistent firm, unifying, loving, insightful, well-read words and actions. Being well-read is essential, as nothing deters winning a battle as an uninformed fighter. We must be aware of the opponent being fought. We are not fighting each other, neither are we battling individual incidents. Instead, we are combating a crashing, colossal calamity that is the crumbling cosmic crisis that was the worldwide colonial cataclysmic test. Every opportunity to calmly confront this beast is valuable. In honor of the ancestors who suffered in the past, some of us are writing, some are speaking, and some are actively working to effect a more socially just environment for our children of the future.

Get good company and GROW. Grow together in understanding and empathy each day. Strive to shine the light inwardly as we shine the light systemically and ask: Are some of my behaviors steeped in conscious or unconscious biases? Am I aligned with a group that helps me to advance within the organization via honest, organizational evaluation? Are organizations/houses of worship/communities to which I belong embracing traditions and behaviors that harm others? Are we giving voice to the marginalized? Are we creating psychological, physical, professional safe zones together? Healthy organizations ask those questions and groom teams that feel comfortable openly answering them.

Hold yourself and others accountable as we examine and heal from wounds caused by professional and societal pain of prejudice and dregs of the botched and barbaric worldwide colonialism and enslavement that left whole nations and thus, organizations, functioning as their microcosms, harmed...thankfully, not irreparably. This means that we do not put others' 'skin-colored' bandages on gaping and festering historic and social wounds. Accountability requires us to ask the hard questions that help us to get to the root of our issues so that we may address them. Among those questions to be asked are: "Am I part of the group that perhaps, speaks the gospel of diversity and inclusion publicly, but privately and among friends perpetuates myths about Black and Brown people? For example: Do I make comments in jest or seriousness such as: "I don't live/work/play/ workout/worship, where (Black people) live, because it's too ghetto, violent, or low class?" Then I must face the fact that I may not yet be a part of the solution. I am a part of the problem.

Take Action: The most important action is to care for yourself. Decide if remaining in that organization or mental space is safe for you to grow. Examine the situation and ask yourself: Is this situation toxic? Am I being bullled...or am I the bully? Is this an exercise in ego and theophobia for someone? Then set healthy boundaries. Resist toxicity by addressing it via your HR Department or legal means if necessary, or at least directly and calmly in the mirror, or with colleagues who are consciously or unconsciously dispensing venomously biased behavior. Try to avoid knee jerk reactions that could negatively affect the career and lifestyle you wish to build. Instead, weigh and strategize a response that conveys your discomfort and helps you to regain your power in your situation. Some unhealthy environments will continue to pretend to change or justify traumatic, biased behavior. Those places require you to plan an exit that is advantageous to you.

To those who have endured organizational trauma, know that you are not alone. Seek others who understand your pain and stand with you in your healing. Together, build social, worship, and professional places of genuine care and belonging sanctuaries against injustice where diversity is cherished and all feel truly seen, heard, and supported. United in shared purpose, we can advocate fiercely yet compassionately for the inclusive, nurturing environments we all deserve. Aboagye, in this way, our courage and resilience can forge a brighter path.

BIO

As founder and leader of consulting firm Talawah Turf International, Dr. Sherone Smith-Sanchez partners with religious and secular leaders to build individual and team capacity for data-driven community service and engagement. TTI provides grant writing, professional development, technical assistance and coaching focused on developing efficient, evidence-based organizations.

Visit https://talawahturf.com/ to learn more.

9

Black Face: White Coat

Pamela Buchanan, MD

As I stand in the bustling emergency room, my stethoscope around my neck and my white coat bearing the hard-earned "MD" after my name, I can't help but reflect on the journey that brought me here. Growing up in a working-class neighborhood, the dream of becoming a doctor seemed both audacious and distant. Yet, fueled by a passion for science and a deep-seated desire to help others, I pursued that dream with unwavering determination.

My path led me from a predominantly Black high school to a medical school, where I was often the only Black face in a sea of white. From there, I ventured into private practice, seeking to establish myself in a field where people who looked like me were woefully underrepresented. However, the siren call of emergency medicine eventually drew me in, leading to my current role as an ER doctor in rural Missouri.

Unbeknownst to me, this career path would place me at the center of a tumultuous situation: a worldwide pandemic that would challenge the capabilities of our healthcare system, coupled with a racial crisis that would compel America to face its entrenched prejudices.

As a Black female doctor in a politically conservative area, I found myself navigating not just the complexities of emergency medicine, but also the treacherous waters of racism and sexism in a profession that ironically prides itself on objectivity and care.

CONFRONTING RACISM IN MEDICINE

The challenges began long before the pandemic, in the supposedly progressive halls of suburban Missouri hospitals. There were the subtle slights: colleagues assuming I was a nurse or support staff, patients questioning my credentials, or the palpable surprise when I demonstrated expertise in complex procedures. Then there were the more overt acts, such as hearing racist jokes in the break room or dealing with patients who openly requested a "different kind of doctor."

But nothing could have prepared me for the heightened racial tensions that emerged during the pandemic. Working as an ER physician and medical director for a rural hospital, I found myself at the forefront of a crisis that disproportionately affected communities of color while simultaneously facing an uptick in racial hostility. The frequency of racial slurs hurled my way increased alarmingly. "I've never been called a nigger more in my life than in those few years of the pandemic," I recall thinking with a mix of anger and exhaustion.

The emotional toll was immense. On certain nights, after a grueling shift of saving lives and battling a relentless virus, I faced the harsh reality that some valued my skin color more than my medical expertise. The constant barrage of microaggressions and outright racism affected my job performance, my mental health, and my passion for medicine.

To survive, I had to develop strategies. I learned to pick my battles, addressing egregious acts of racism while letting smaller slights slide for the sake of my sanity. I sought support from administration when necessary, though I often found their response lacking. Most importantly, I learned to develop a thick skin while still preserving my empathy—a delicate balance crucial for survival in this field.

UNEXPECTED ALLIES: BUILDING BRIDGES ACROSS RACIAL LINES

Amidst the darkness, pinpricks of light emerged in the form of unexpected allies. Despite my initial wariness, I found myself forging meaningful connections with some of my white colleagues. These relationships often started tentatively—a shared eyeroll at a sexist comment, a moment of camaraderie during a particularly tough shift—but gradually evolved into genuine friendships.

The power of female solidarity in our male-dominated field became a lifeline. I found common ground with white female physicians who, while not experiencing racism, understood the sting of gender discrimination. These shared experiences opened doors to deeper conversations about race and privilege.

One particularly memorable moment came during a team-building retreat. As we shared our experiences, I opened up about a recent racist encounter with a patient. The room fell silent, and then, to my surprise, several of my white colleagues spoke up, not to defend or excuse but to listen and validate my experience. That moment of vulnerability and understanding marked a turning point in our relationships.

CAREER ADVANCEMENT THROUGH MENTORSHIP AND SUPPORT

As these friendships deepened, I found myself benefiting from unexpected mentorship and support. Two experiences stand out vividly:

First, a white female colleague advised me to command loan repayment and ask for higher pay. I was initially hesitant, plagued by imposter syndrome and fear of appearing "difficult." But with her encouragement, I negotiated successfully, securing both loan repayment and a significant pay increase.

Second, my ER doctor friend, Randi, pushed me to ask for a $75,000 sign-on bonus when I was considering a new position. The very idea terrified me, but Randi's belief in my worth gave me the courage to ask. To my amazement, they agreed.

These experiences were transformative. Not only did they have immediate financial implications, but they also boosted my confidence and self-advocacy skills. I learned to recognize my worth in the medical field and developed techniques for effective self-advocacy that have served me well throughout my career.

NAVIGATING THE COMPLEXITIES OF RACE IN PROFESSIONAL RELATIONSHIPS

Building these relationships wasn't always easy. Years of experiencing racism had made me cautious, and letting my guard down took time and effort. I had to learn to balance this caution with openness, to identify potential allies without becoming vulnerable to further hurt.

The process involved many honest, often uncomfortable conversations about race. I found myself in the position of educating my colleagues about my experiences as a Black doctor, helping them understand the weight of microaggressions and the impact of systemic racism in healthcare.

These discussions were challenging but ultimately rewarding. They helped bridge racial divides and fostered a more inclusive work environment. More importantly, they reminded me of the power of individual actions in creating systemic change.

LESSONS LEARNED AND PERSONAL GROWTH

This journey has taught me invaluable lessons about resilience, self-care, and the importance of support networks. I've learned to bounce back from racial incidents, to prioritize my mental health, and to build a diverse network of support both within and outside of medicine.

Perhaps most importantly, I've learned to balance the acknowledgment of racism with an appreciation for allies. It's a delicate equilibrium—maintaining a nuanced view of race relations in medicine while avoiding broad generalizations. This balance has been crucial in maintaining my passion for medicine and my hope for positive change.

LOOKING FORWARD: PROMOTING DIVERSITY AND INCLUSION IN MEDICINE

My experiences have fueled a commitment to mentoring other Black medical professionals. I've become involved in formal mentorship programs and make a point of offering guidance to young Black doctors navigating similar challenges.

I've also become an advocate for change within healthcare institutions. Through involvement in diversity initiatives and policy committees, I push for concrete actions to create more inclusive environments. This work is ongoing and often frustrating, but it's a crucial part of creating the change I want to see in medicine.

REFLECTING ON PROGRESS AND CHALLENGES

As I look back on my journey, I'm proud of the progress I've made and the challenges I've overcome. From that young girl dreaming of becoming a doctor to the emergency medicine physician I am today, each step has been a testament to resilience and determination.

Yet, I'm acutely aware that the need for racial equity in medicine persists. The challenges I've faced are not unique to me, and many barriers remain for Black professionals in healthcare.

Despite this, I remain hopeful. My positive experiences with allies remind me of the power of individual actions in creating change.

To my fellow minority professionals, I say: persist, advocate for yourself, and don't be afraid to lean on your support network. To potential allies, I urge: listen, educate yourselves, and use your privilege to amplify marginalized voices.

The path to true equity in medicine is long, but with each step, each conversation, and each act of allyship, we move closer to a healthcare system that truly serves and represents all. As we continue this journey, let us remember that our ultimate goal—providing compassionate, quality care to all patients—is what unites us, transcending the divisions of race, gender, or background.

BIO

Dr. Pamela Buchanan is a board-certified physician with over 20 years of experience in private practice and emergency medicine.

A TEDx speaker and ambassador for the Lorna Beene Foundation, she is also the author of Emotional Flatline and a contributor to the anthology Triumph in the Trenches: Navigating Success for Black Professionals Volume 2.

Dr. Buchanan earned her undergraduate degree from Washington University and went on to study at Ross University School of Medicine. She completed her residency at Mercy Hospital in St. Louis, Missouri, where she has lived her entire life.

Known for her effortless connection with people, she takes great pride in understanding her patients. A mother of three, she enjoys traveling and reading in her spare time.

Learn more at https://www.strongmedicinestl.com/.

10

Foundations for Change

Phillip Woolfolk

n the first volume of *Triumph in The Trenches, Navigating Success for Black Professionals,* I wrote about Fighting Corporate Style. I referenced one of my lived experiences, as my fellow co-authors did from their various perspectives and their lived experiences as well. We collectively shared how we triumphed in the trenches and successfully navigated through our many different work environments, across many sectors. Those sectors included corporate, private, public, and non-profit sectors alike. What we discovered was that our collective experiences were common realities in whatever environment in which we found ourselves. I believe this commonality rings true to so many as we discovered we are not alone. Therefore, as we confronted micro-aggressions, systemic racism, sexism, classism and other barriers, each of the lived experiences resonated profoundly with our many readers across the United States and abroad. The feedback, testimonials, and comments from readers indicated that many of them genuinely identified with the lived experiences of each of the anthologists.

As I pondered examining the idea of Fighting Corporate Style 2.0, I pondered our community at-large including women, people of color, low-and moderate-income people, the differently-abled, and others who may find themselves in this huge group of underserved, under-utilized, and under- performing, largely due to being under-resourced, many of whom may be collectively referred to as minorities.

However, by placing human beings in different buckets, the power elite gets to play the role of majority and, through ongoing strategies of colonialization resulting in the control of natural resources, amasses enormous fortunes for the privileged few. Upon this, they build a legacy of wealth while relegating the true majority to a legacy of poverty and mediocrity, where a smaller percentage of successes stand out as an example of what's possible, even with the proverbial deck stacked against them.

This stacking of the deck to which I am referring is maintained through systems, policies and practices including but not limited to the political process of legislation, judicial appointments at the supreme court, appellate courts, other areas of the judicial process, law enforcement, mass incarceration, removing Black and Brown males from the home, virtually ensuring the loss of a critical element of success for families through incarceration with disparate sentencing for comparative crimes and the sentencing of others. Then there are the corporate, private, public, and non-profit spaces, where systems, policies and practices are also in place to ensure the status quo. And when efforts are brought forward to improve the situation and balance the scales of equity and inclusion, there are legal efforts to roll those efforts back, as the European male community screams reverse discrimination, after over 400 years of being privileged with historical advantages, too numerous to mention.

One such example is the action taken against the Fearless Fund. Fearless Fund is a venture capital firm, seeking to close the access to capital gap for Black entrepreneurs. A lawsuit was brought forth by the American Alliance for Equal Rights (AAER), claiming Fearless Fund's Striver's Grant Contest, which was open "only to Black females," was discriminatory. Ultimately, Fearless Fund dropped the grant program to settle the lawsuit.

To that end, I must sarcastically report that The American Alliance for Equal Rights (AAER), must not have been made aware of the New Jersey Disparity Study covering the period of 2015-2020, wherein there is huge disparity in contracts awarded, with Black entrepreneurs at the bottom in every category. But, perhaps the true concern was not "equal rights."

I would suspect if that were really the concern there would have been a claim filed against the State of New Jersey. To my knowledge, no such claim has been filed, perhaps it's because the bulk of the billions in state contracts during the study period went to European American men, and the second largest group of contracts went to the "other minority", European-American women-owned businesses.

As I look back historically at the Civil Rights Movement, the next major campaign Dr. Martin Luther King, Jr. and the Southern Christian Leadership Conference (SCLC) was slated to embark on was the Poor People's Campaign. As a unified movement, this could have been a force to be reckoned with if not for all the forces that masterfully separate and divide people. It is a time-honored weapon of "divide and conquer." The colonization of much of the Black and Brown parts of the world to the benefit of a relatively small minority is a prime example.

We must keep all of this in perspective, considering the many challenges and barriers we have faced historically as African Americans. This is a subset of the many who may also be impacted. I find it amazing that on one hand there are monumental criticisms about our lack of broad-scale success, and yet the systems deployed go back to the Federal Housing Administration's policy and practice of legally denying African Americans the right to use the systems others had access to for the simple purchase of a home. To put it simply, African Americans were denied the ability to purchase homes with an FHA mortgage. One such covenant identified as a "Declaration of Restrictions," referring to a deeded property. This example was included in a builder's 1970 excerpt from a document in California, which appears as follows:

"The real property above described, or any portion thereof, shall never be occupied, used or resided on by any person not of the white or Caucasian race, except in the capacity of a servant or domestic employed thereon as such by a white Caucasian owner, tenant or occupant."

This system and practice of equity, asset, and wealth suppression was fully endorsed by the U.S. Government and enforced by the same. Richard Rothstein addresses this topic more fully in his book, *The Color of Law*.

Throughout the nation, courts ordered African Americans to be evicted from homes they had purchased. Restrictive covenants were incorporated in deeds and those covenants were enforced by governments at all levels, promoting and enforcing laws and practices that to this day negatively impact the wealth basis of African Americans. Home ownership created generational wealth for the families who were afforded the opportunity to purchase homes and build equity. That equity provided a resource for those privileged to access it, to educate their children, fund their businesses, invest in markets and in general build a legacy of wealth, while others were forced into a legacy of poverty, with systemic barriers to hold as many there as possible for generations post slavery and reconstruction.

Contrary to the propaganda we have been bombarded with, the wealth gap does not exist because an entire race of people is lazy. The same people who played a major role, through the profits produced from their free labor, as they participated as enslaved people in various slave industries, ultimately building the country into an economic superpower. Additionally, many of its long-standing institutions, including institutions of higher learning, benefited as well.

For example, the "early benefactors who gave money to Brown and Harvard universities made their fortunes running slave ships to Africa and milling cotton from plantations in the American South; "Georgetown could afford to offer free tuition to its earliest students by virtue of the unpaid labor of its Jesuit-owned slaves on plantations in Maryland"; the University of Virginia was "founded and designed by Thomas Jefferson whose slaves cooked and cleaned for the sons of the Southern gentry"; " Yale inherited a plantation in Rhode Island that it used to fund its first graduate programs and its first scholarships; Princeton University was founded in 1746.

As indicated in its own research, Princeton was intertwined between liberty and slavery. "Princeton educated leaders of America's fight for independence, hosted the Continental Congress in 1783 and yet the first nine of its presidents all owned slaves." We are now to believe, those whose ancestors provided labor as enslaved people, would pass on DNA to those who are suddenly too lazy to work toward getting ahead. I would retort very simply that the same people who have been marginalized and minimized could have easily been millionaires and billionaires alike, had they been afforded the opportunity to have free labor, upon which to build their fortunes, institutions, and legacies. Therefore, those who have built those fortunes do not necessarily possess some unique set of genius characteristics, which sets them apart or above any others.

HAND UP OR HAND OUT?

For example, the Homestead Act of 1862 was a law that provided 160 acres of public land to citizens (white settlers) and intended citizens (European immigrants), who would live on and improve the land. Some of which came with timber, gas, oil, and other mineral rights, contributing to generational wealth for many of those families. This law helped develop the American West and spur economic growth for that part of the country.

This distribution of wealth amounted to 270 million acres. This served as a leg up, a foundation upon which to build, while the descendants of the enslaved people, who were the contributors and pawns of wealth who provided free labor to create what we now see as institutional and generational wealth with no inheritance from the ancestral labor. In fact, instead of the potential of being trust fund babies, our generation is left with what Dr. King referred to as that promissory note in his "I Have a Dream" speech as a metaphor to describe the Constitution and the Declaration of Independence. I use it here as a metaphor for the promise of the 40-acres and a mule.

As such, neither the 40-acres nor the mule has ever materialized, that promissory note also has come back marked insufficient funds.

While others received a hand up on the front side of life, reparations on the back side of the labor of our ancestors is yet to materialize. In fact, reparations is one of those conversations that yield evil stares and nasty comments as if the U.S Government has not done it before or since. We could easily conclude that the bail outs of the auto industry and banking industries were huge forms of corporate welfare or reparations. Call it what you will, those industries got to use taxpayer dollars to rebuild and strengthen themselves and in cases where they repaid the funding, they did so with other people's money.

And let's not forget about corporate tax incentives, corporate tax abatements, funding the wars of foreign governments amounting to trillions of dollars, as the struggle continues to pay interest on the federal debt. While Black Farmers still struggle to gain access to the same support their Caucasian counterparts have received for their agricultural endeavors. And yet, funding healthcare, social security, and other initiatives to take care of all U.S. citizens takes the back seat, as the concern for budget deficits rear their ugly head when the subject of domestic spending is broached, especially to support the underserved and under resourced. Of course, many of these efforts are necessary in moderation and managing the federal deficit is an important agenda item for our elected officials. In my opinion, there needs to be a balanced approach to how it all gets distributed in the name of fairness and equity. But of course, many of those corporate entities were and are today considered too big, and too essential to the economy to fail.

So, as we reflect on some of the disparities that have historical significance, we remain confronted in the present day by barriers and challenges imposed on the least of thee to maintain the status quo. These barriers and systemic practices impact the wealth gap in many ways such as public contracts.

To that end and as an example, I spent about 4-years as Treasurer of the African American Chamber of Commerce of New Jersey (AACCNJ) and a little over 3-years as its Chief Operations Officer. The Founder, President, and CEO of the Chamber spent a number of years advocating for a disparity study to be done in New Jersey. That study was finally completed in January of 2024. The hope and expectation are for all of the public agencies in the state of New Jersey to use the dismal results of the disparity study to establish much needed goals. AACCNJ's Disparity Task Force has made credible legislative and executive order type recommendations with the express goal to close the massive disparity gaps. The study covered a five-year period from 2015-2020. By way of example, for construction contracts Black owned businesses received approximately $3.3 million compared to White-male owned businesses who received $10.8 billion. In the area of professional services Black-owned companies received $13.7 million in contracts compared to White-owned businesses who received $3.4 billion in contracts. It will take a monumental effort to close the disparity gap. Additionally, the elected officials, and civil servants who administer the procurement process must be held mutually accountable to turn around the dismal results of the study.

I find it extremely interesting that the environment of the 1960's brought forth the idea for the Poor People's Campaign under the leadership of Dr. Martin Luther King, Jr. and as we fast forward to 2024 in New Jersey, one of the most diverse states in the nation, a state in which you would expect things to be more equitable and fairer, not one in which African American businesses still find themselves at the bottom, with very little economic reciprocity for its political support in the state at the ballot box. Having served on Governor Murphy's Transition Team, I witnessed firsthand the promise of "fairer," which included equity and inclusivity.

And almost 8 years later, the rhetoric has not translated into intentionality with real goals for fundamental fairness, equity, and the desire to create wealth through public sector contracts. For those who have been systematically unable to fully participate in the economic mainstream it is the common thread between the inspired dreams of the 1960's and the present-day disappointments, as evidenced in New Jersey by the results of the 2024 New Jersey Disparity Study over 60-years later.

Time will tell whether the legislative body, the governor, civil servants and others have the intestinal fortitude to act on the results they claimed to have been waiting for in order to have a legal basis upon which to make necessary changes in the form of tangible, enforceable goals with incentives and accountability measures to foster success, including penalties for non-compliance.

We do know that New Jersey is but a microcosm of a larger picture of disparity. Fortunately, there are some states that have made significant strides to build equity and create wealth in a much more inclusive way in their public contracting and procurement protocols. New York and California come to mind as demonstrating best practices that others can glean from, if they are serious about closing the disparity gaps. It is my sincere hope that change is coming soon in all the areas of the country where change is needed and the best practices can serve to shorten the time needed for such changes and improvements. Fundamental fairness and equity will build our global competitiveness as we all rise together.

In addition, we must also look at how the African American Community handles the resources with which it has and how we might address this area from the standpoint of self-improvement.

Suffice it to say, the African American community has to make better use of its collective economic power. One simple way to achieve this is to shop where the culture, causes, and commitments to the community are evident through the good corporate citizenship of the companies that benefit from their share of the Black dollar.

Before I get to that, I would like to briefly define my concept of Fighting Corporate Style. In the first book, I shared the applied lessons from the street that I was able to apply in the workplace during my career in banking. I have also been able to apply some of those lessons as an entrepreneur, a real estate investor, professional manager and in other areas of my life's journey.

For me, fighting corporate style is simply making decisions that are void of emotions like anger, violence, frustration, depression, despair, reactionism, and unprofessionalism. It is being slow to anger, thinking strategically about what you want the outcome to be and then to be hyper-focused on positioning oneself to successfully implement and execute a plan that gets the desired result(s).

For example, the day after the 2024 presidential election, Dr. Deforest Soaries, retired pastor of First Baptist Church of Lincoln Gardens and founder of the D-Free Movement and the D-Free Global Foundation, hosted what I will call the What's Next Webinar. One of the things he articulated that fully resonated with me was the fact that, "anger, frustration, despair, and depression are not strategies." Additionally, and regardless of the outcome of this election or any other, there needs to be a strategy for "what's next." I will offer some of my ideas of what I believe will move the community in the right direction.

AFRICAN AMERICAN PURCHASING POWER

Now back to our collective economic power and my view of it. A good friend, Kymberly Graham, an executive at Nielsen IQ, tracks, monitors, and does an excellent job presenting Nielsen IQ's data. In a recent presentation she shared, the African American consumer spend has reached approximately $1.8 trillion dollars as of 2024. Black consumers represent about 14% of the population. And yet command a purchasing power that rivals the GDP of many nations. If this demographic were a nation, it would be not far behind Brazil which was estimated at $2.17 trillion in 2023 according to the World Bank, and not far behind Russia, whose GDP was estimated to be $ 2.02 trillion in 2023 and slightly ahead of Mexico's GDP, which was estimated at $1.789 trillion in 2023.

It has been said that the African American community does not have a money problem, but a unity problem. There is plenty of data to argue this point from different sides of this both pro and con. However, purely from a spend point of view there is a lack of return on investment as our consumer spending does not bring forth equity, assets, or provide any on-going revenue or cash flow. Some of the spending is simply on brands which provide a sense of living the American dream defined by material wealth, such as luxury cars, designer clothing, and jewelry. Typically, these kinds of purchases provide an appearance of wealth without the substance real wealth brings. In order to make real progress in this area there needs to be a shift toward building a financial foundation by focusing on financial education, asset growth, cash flow, wealth building, financial legacy, estate planning for the next generation, expanding philanthropic support for causes that benefit the long-term viability our community including, domestic financial well-being, and investment on the African continent.

For example, the top two categories of spending include salty snacks and soft drinks. Blacks and Hispanics outspend Whites by 30% on clothing, cars, and jewelry. The bottom line on the spending is to reallocate a portion of the $1.8 trillion dollar spend to build equity and wealth. For example, reallocation could include business acquisition, business partnerships, real estate, dividend paying stocks, real estate investment trusts, cash value life insurance, and other opportunities to build a portfolio of appreciating assets versus depreciating assets such as new cars, the renting of luxury apartments, and purchasing of brands and supporting organizations that neither respect or support our culture or causes important to our community.

There also needs to be a movement toward manufacturing some of the products the African American community consumes. By having a market share position, resources can be recycled in the community in the form of employment opportunities, training, and internships. This would solidify a more equitable financial future. One in which the causes of our community's long-term growth and development are a primary focus.

STRATEGIES AND TACTICS TO CONSIDER

It all starts with mutual respect and mutual benefit. For example, while in high school, I played flute in the pep band at school sporting events. I had a part-time job, and I took part of my weekly pay to buy music, in the form of albums back then. On one occasion, I purchased an album and when I got home to listen to the music, I discovered the album was scratched and the damage did not provide a good listening experience. The next day after school, I returned to the record shop to exchange the album. Unfortunately, I was met with utter disrespect by the owner of the shop. So when I got home, I wrote the owner a letter. In the letter, I explained that I was in the pep band at high school, and my musical friends and I shopped regularly in his store on a weekly basis. My 10th grade class had approximately 1500 students, and I was appalled by the treatment I received when attempting to return a damaged album. I went on to articulate that if the matter was not resolved satisfactorily, I would be happy to share my experience with my entire high school and urge all of them to move our business to the other record store down the street. I dropped that letter in the mail and in a few days, when I got home from school, my mother shared that the record store owner had called asking for Mr. Woolfolk. I returned his call and was invited to the store for the exchange. I took several friends so the owner could see that we were in his store regularly.

The first thing he said to me was you cannot threaten a man's business the way I had indicated I would in my letter. However, my friends and I all got a couple of free albums that day. I learned from this experience that just like fighting the bullies growing up, bullies are everywhere, and they seem pretty tough until they get punched in the nose. Letting the store owner know there would be repercussions for mistreating a loyal customer was fighting corporate style and my way of punching him in the nose. He did not care about me individually, but he did care about the possible economic impact of 100s of young people by passing his store every week to shop elsewhere.

We are not powerless. Being part of a $1.8 trillion purchasing group gives us power, which we must use to be respected and demand market changes. If more Black representation is wanted on corporate boards, more in c-suite, more recruitment on Black college campuses, more corporate dollars spent with Black owned firms, this is a strategy that may provide some measure of success.

WHAT CAN YOU DO?

Become more intentional with your spending, saving, investing, and philanthropy. Transition away from companies that transition away from diversity on their corporate boards, executive leadership ranks, recruitment from Black college campuses and HBCU's, and do not exhibit a propensity for spending with Black owned companies.

Take 50% of your discretionary dollars and invest it. This might include what is spent on coffee at high-end coffee shops, salty snacks, soft drinks, fast foods, cigarettes, alcohol, adult/recreational marijuana, that third, fourth, and 5th watch or jewelry, and any unplanned impulse purchase.

It is important to hold all elected officials accountable for the community-beneficial commitments they make while running for office, and to measure them equally, regardless of their person or party affiliation. Did they deliver?

If you work for a company that offers a 401-K, 403-B for non-profits, fully participate to take advantage of any company match offered. Stop leaving money on the table so you can get the maximum company match and grow your wealth.

Save and invest 100% of any bonus or pay increase. Begin participating in the stock market. You do not have to be a trained stock picker, develop a portfolio based on products you have in your house that are good companies that you trust. Some of them are legacy dividend paying companies.

If you work and have a "good job," start a business and as your income grows, use those additional funds to build a financial fortress to grow your wealth basis, independent of the J-O-B. Develop a strategy to live beneath your means. You do not want to live on and spend every dollar that flows through your hands. Educate yourself to become more financially literate. The 12 Steps to Financial Freedom, an excellent guide from the Dfree Foundation, Inc., can assist you in your journey. In fact, please consider the Dfree foundation in your personal and corporate Phil-anthropic plans by visiting dfreefoundation.org and making a contribution.

We must unite our organizations around political, social, and economic paradigms, both domestically and throughout the diaspora. We must build unity around resources and opportunities on the continent of Africa, moving toward investment, equity, employment, and entrepreneurship for our community as a whole.

In closing, develop the skills necessary to begin Fighting Corporate Style for the benefit of your family and your community. This will serve to gain the respect you deserve in the marketplace, as you let your dollars speak for you by how you manage your resources. And one thing for sure is the fact that the business world understands dollars and it's up to you to make sure your dollars make sense.

BIO

Phillip serves as Managing Director of Phillip Speaks, LLC and Main Street Advisory, LLC.

Through Phillip Speaks, LLC, Phillip serves as a speaker for in-person and virtual meetings, webinars, workshops, events, and conferences. Some of the topics include access to capital, empowerment, business growth, and sustainability. Other topics are enumerated on the website. Book a call with Phillip to discuss your project for consideration. As an Author, both "Triumph In The Trenches, Navigating Success For Black Professionals", and "Volume 2" can ordered on the website.be ordered on the website https://www.PhillipWoolfolk.com.

Through Main Street Advisory, Phillip serves as an Alternative Lender facilitating funding for real estate investors, builders, developers, and entrepreneurs needing equipment, working capital, and start-up funding. Visit the website to learn more: https://www.MainStreetAdvisoryLLC.com.

Phillip's background includes the banking industry where he started as teller, then foreign teller, head teller, financial services representative, sales manager, commercial, small business and development manager for residential mortgage lending, and vice president and fair lending manager for a seven-state market area. In the non-profit space Phillip served as the chief operations officer for the African American Chamber of Commerce of New Jersey, chief administrative officer for Granville Charter School, and retail manager for a federal credit union. As a volunteer he has served as board chairman, board treasurer, committee chair, and board member.

Currently, Phillip serves on the boards of the for-profit parent company of US Medical Innovations, LLC, Villa Victoria Academy, Oceans Harbor House, and chairs the credit committee for New Jersey Community Capital, a community development financial institution. He has also served as an honorary commander with the US Airforce at McGuire, Dix-Lakehurst. He has also served as the Founder and Co-owner of a real estate investment company.

Additionally, Phillip served on the New Jersey Governor's Transition team in 2018, participating in the Stronger and Fairer Economy Committee, Encouraging Ownership, and the Inclusive Growth Sub-Committees. Phillip has been married for 36 years, and he and his family reside in Mercer County, New Jersey.

NAVIGATING WORKPLACE BIASES AND POLITICS

1. How have you navigated workplace dynamics that challenge your identity, and what strategies have helped you advocate for yourself?

_____

_____

_____

_____

_____

_____

_____

_____

_____

_____

_____

_____

_____

_____

_____

_____

_____

_____

2. How have workplace biases—whether implicit or explicit—impacted your career growth, and what strategies can you use to challenge or navigate them effectively?

_____

_____

_____

_____

_____

_____

_____

_____

_____

_____

_____

_____

_____

_____

_____

_____

_____

_____

_____

_____

MAINTAINING MENTAL WELLNESS AT WORK

1. What steps can you take to protect your mental health while maintaining authenticity in spaces that may not fully embrace you?

_____

_____

_____

_____

_____

_____

_____

_____

_____

_____

_____

_____

_____

_____

_____

_____

2. How does your work environment impact your emotional well-being, and what boundaries can you set to foster balance and resilience?

_____

_____

_____

_____

_____

_____

_____

_____

_____

_____

_____

_____

_____

_____

_____

_____

_____

_____

_____

_____

_____

CREATING FINANCIAL FREEDOM BEYOND THE 9-TO-5

1. What financial strategies can you implement today to create long-term security and reduce reliance on traditional employment?

_____

_____

_____

_____

_____

_____

_____

_____

_____

_____

_____

_____

_____

_____

_____

_____

_____

_____

2. How can collective economic empowerment within your community help shift generational wealth and financial stability?

_____

_____

_____

_____

_____

_____

_____

_____

_____

_____

_____

_____

_____

_____

_____

_____

_____

_____

_____

Continue Your Journey

Thank you for taking the time to immerse yourself in these stories. If this book spoke to you, if it inspired, comforted, or challenged you in meaningful ways, we invite you to explore more.

Visit www.theauthorsjourney.co/books to discover similar books and join The Author's Journey Reader's List.

Each story we publish is crafted with care, meant to light a path and remind us of our shared humanity.

It's never too late to journey toward healing, authenticity, and transformation.

Bibliography

"Aboagye: Name Meaning, Origin & More | MyloFamily." 2018. Mylo. 2018. https://mylofamily.com/parenting/babynames/meaning-of-aboagye-8416.

Adler, Ronald B., Lawrence B Rosenfeld, Neil Towne, and Russell F Proctor. 2004. Interplay : The Process of Interpersonal Communication. New York; Oxford: Oxford University Press.

American Psychological Association. (2013). How stress affects your health. https://www.apa.org/topics/stress/health.

Campbell, Katie. 2021. "Black and Asian Solidarity: 20 Artists Explore America's Complicated Relationship with Race." Kuow.org. KUOW Public Radio. June 8, 2021. https://www.kuow.org/stories/black-and-asian-solidarity-how-20-artists-explored-america-s-complicated-relationship-with-race.

Center for Creative Leadership. (2024). The Importance of Empathy in the Workplace. https://www.ccl.org/articles/leading-effectively-articles/empathy-in-the-workplace-a-tool-for-effective-leadership/.

Chang, Michael and David Aaronson, "Barriers to Workplace Accommodation: A Mixed-Methods Analysis," *Disability Studies Quarterly* 43, no. 1 (2023): 72-89.

Chen, Aaron. "Neurodiversity in Tech: Unleashing Innovation through Inclusive Practices," *MIT Sloan Management Review* 65, no. 3 (2024): 217.

Cho, Elaine. "The Accommodation Battleground: Navigating Disability Rights in the Modern Workplace," *Harvard Business Review* 100, no. 2 (2022): 43.

Crawford, C. M. (2024). Understanding Mental Health in Black Communities. McLean Hospital. https://www.mcleanhospital.org/essential/black-mental-health

Crawshaw, Laura. 2023. Grow Your Spine & Manage Abrasive Leadership Behavior: A Guide for Those Who Manage Bosses Who Bully. New York, New York: Executive Insight Press.

Darden-Robinson, Mary. 2024. Triumph in the Trenches Volume: Navigating Success for Black Professionals. Nashville, Tennessee: The Author's Journey.

Degruy, Joy and Randall Robinson. 2005. Post Traumatic Slave Syndrome: America's Legacy of Enduring Injury and Healing. United States: Joy Degruy Publications Inc.

Gandolfi, Franco and Seth Stone. "Toxic leadership: Behaviors, characteristics, and consequences." Journal of Management Research 22, no. 1 (2022): 19-27.

Garcia, Lisa and Robert Thompson, "Redefining Productivity: Neurodiversity and the Future of Work," *Academy of Management Journal* 67, no. 1 (2024): 112.

"Gun Violence Survivors in America." n.d. Everytown Research & Policy. https://everytownresearch.org/report/gun-violence-survivors-america/.

Hogan Assessments. (2023). The State of Leadership 2023. https://www.hoganassessments.com/wp-content/uploads/2023/04/State-of-Leadership-2023.pdf

"Intimate Partner Violence and Mental Health Outcomes Among Black Women," *American Journal of Public Health* 113, no. 4 (2022): 45-52.

Ling, Yumi, Kenji Sato, and Thomas Brown, "Neurodiversity and Team Performance: A Longitudinal Study," *Journal of Applied Psychology* 107, no. 4 (2022): 583–599.

Magazine, Authority. 2023. "Laura Crawshaw of the Boss Whispering Institute on How Managers & Team Leaders Can Help Eliminate Workplace Bullying and Harassment." Medium. Authority Magazine. July 7, 2023. https://medium.com/authority-magazine/laura-crawshaw-of-the-boss-whispering-institute-on-how-managers-team-leaders-can-help-eliminate-1e170a8b0fd7.

Maria Szulc, Joanna, Julie Davies, Michał T. Tomczak, and Frances-Louise McGregor. 2021. "AMO Perspectives on the Well-Being of Neurodivergent Human Capital." Employee Relations: The International Journal 43 (4): 858–72. https://doi.org/10.1108/er-09-2020-0446.

Mass General Brigham McLean. 2022. "Understanding Mental Health in Black Communities | McLean Hospital." Www.mcleanhospital.org. McLean Hospital. November 8, 2022. https://www.mcleanhospital.org/essential/black-mental-health.

McKinsey & Company, "Women in the Workplace: Black Women and Mental Health Accommodations" (New York: McKinsey & Company, 2023), 15.

"Microaggressions." n.d. Obo. https://www.oxfordbibliographies.com/display/document/obo-9780199828340/obo-9780199828340-0310.xml.

MIT Sloan Management Review. (2023). Toxic Culture Gap Shows Companies Are Failing Women. https://sloanreview.mit.edu/article/toxic-culture-gap-shows-companies-are-failing-women/.

"National Inventor's Day: Marjorie S. Joyner." 2019. National Archives Museum. 2019. https://visit.archives.gov/whats-on/explore-exhibits/national-inventors-day-marjorie-s-joyner.

National Health Service. 2022. "Symptoms - Post-Traumatic Stress Disorder." Nhs.uk. NHS. May 13, 2022. https://www.nhs.uk/mental-health/conditions/post-traumatic-stress-disorder-ptsd/symptoms/.

National Partnership for Women & Families, "Domestic Violence's Impact on Women's Economic Security" (Washington, DC: National Partnership for Women & Families, 2022), 12.

Patel, Rajesh. Thriving Together: The Psychology of Inclusive Workplaces* (Oxford: Oxford University Press, 2023), 276.

Roberson, Quinetta, Ann Marie Ryan, and Belle Rose Ragins. 2017. "The Evolution and Future of Diversity at Work." Journal of Applied Psychology 102 (3): 483–99.

Robinson, Cheryl. 2024. "Could You Be a Toxic Leader? Here's How to Know." Forbes, August 29, 2024. https://www.forbes.com/sites/cherylrobinson/2024/08/28/could-you-be-a-toxic-leader-heres-how-to-know/.

Society for Human Resource Management. (2024). Black Employees Discuss Effects of Hostile Work Environments. https://www.shrm.org/topics-tools/news/inclusion-diversity/black-employees-discuss-effects-of-hostile-work-environments.

Society for Human Resource Management, "Race and Gender Disparities in Workplace Accommodations" (Alexandria, VA: SHRM, 2023), 28.

Society for Human Resource Management. (2019). The High Cost of a Toxic Workplace Culture. https://www.shrm.org/hr-today/trends-and-forecasting/research-and-surveys/Pages/SHRM-Culture-Report.aspx.

Stenberg, Mark. 2023. "Black-Owned Publishers Are Building More Collaborative Collective Models to Court Brand Budgets." Adweek.com. Adweek. October 30, 2023. https://www.adweek.com/media/black-owned-publishers-are-building-more-collaborative-collective-models-to-court-brand-budgets/.

Stergiopoulos, Erene, Adriana Cimo, Chiachen Cheng, Sarah Bonato, and Carolyn S Dewa. 2011. "Interventions to Improve Work Outcomes in Work-Related PTSD: A Systematic Review." BMC Public Health 11 (1). https://doi.org/10.1186/1471-2458-11-838.

Sull, Donald, Charles Sull, and Ben Zweig. 2022. "Toxic Culture Is Driving the Great Resignation." MIT Sloan Management Review. January 11, 2022. https://sloanreview.mit.edu/article/toxic-culture-is-driving-the-great-resignation/.

Taylor, Jasmine. "Unmasking at Work: The Cost of Conformity for Neurodivergent Employees," *Journal of Occupational Health Psychology* 28, no. 1 (2023): 92.

"The Psychological Effects of Micromanagement." n.d. Psychvarsity. https://www.psychvarsity.com/Psychological-Effects-Of-Micromanagement.

The State of Workplace Injustice Report a Fact Sheet of Workplace Injustice in America." n.d. https://antongunn.com/wp-content/uploads/2024/06/Workplace-Injustice-in-America_-A-Summary-Fact-Sheet-.pdf.

Urban Institute, "Community Violence and Mental Health: Impact on Black Women" (Washington, DC: Urban Institute, 2023), 31.

Wong, Michael and Emily Silverman, *The Disability Inclusion Advantage: Linking Inclusion to Corporate Performance* (New York: Accenture, 2024), 45.

Yoon, Hyejin, Minjung Choi, and Ayoung Suh, "Presence versus Performance: A Meta-Analysis of Flexible Work Arrangements and Productivity," *Human Resource Management Review* 32, no. 1 (2022): 100845.

www.ingramcontent.com/pod-product-compliance
Lightning Source LLC
Chambersburg PA
CBHW060426130626
46555CB00005B/2228